Practical English for Flight Attendants

   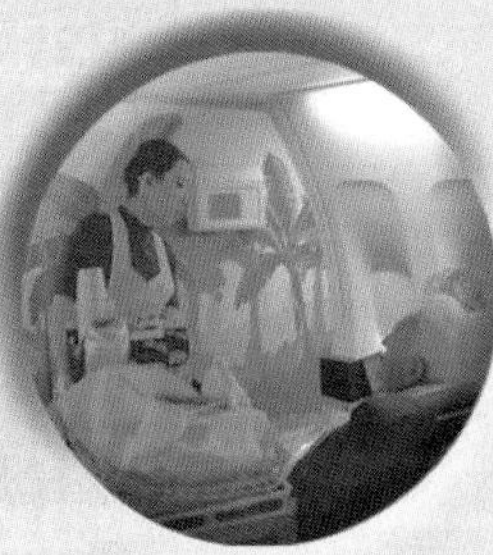 

Hyon-sue Kim
Reashelle Braiden

B/S Publishing Co.

AUTHOR

• Hyon-sue Kim(김 현 수)

경희대학교 영어영문학 학사/석사/박사
Brookdale Community College (New Jersey, U.S.A.) 수료
Berlitz Language School (Ohio, U.S.A.) Translater
장안대학 관광외국어계열 영어통역과 교수 (1983~현재)

〈저서〉

Tourism English Reading
English Reading for College Student
Reading Adventure
Situational Conversation (공저)
Prospective English Reading (공저)
Essential English (공저)

〈논문〉

즈네뜨(G. Genette)의 시간이론으로 본 포크너(Wm. Faulkner)의
〈압살롬, 압살롬!〉(Absalom, Absalom!)외 다수

• Reashelle Braiden

Bachelor of Arts, The University of Winnipeg (Winnipeg, Canada)
Professor, Department of Tourism English Translation
Jangan College

Practical English for Flight Attendants

Baek-san Publishing Co.
370, Hoedong-gil, Paju-si, Gyeonggi-do,
#413-150 Korea

ISBN 978-89-7739-931-0 92740

Printed in Korea 2007. 1. 30. Second edition 2009.2.18. Third edition 2.20. Fourth edition 2013.8.25.
Fifth edition 2015.9.10

※ 저자와 합의로 인지첩부 생략함.
※ 책값은 뒤표지에 있습니다(Audio CD 포함).

Introduction

국제회의 및 각종 문화 이벤트, 글로벌 비즈니스 등으로 인해 급속도로 활발해진 국제 교류와 관광객의 증가로 인해 한국을 찾는 외국인들이 많아지고 있다. 여러 가지 다양한 상황 속에서 일어나는, 그리고 다양한 외국인들의 요구에 부응하는 유창한 영어 커뮤니케이션 능력을 갖춘 승무원들이 절실히 요구된다.

이 책은 flight attendant를 목표로 공부하고 있는 학생들이나, 항공 서비스업과 관련된 직업에 종사하는 전문인들이 보다 훌륭한 서비스를 수행하기 위하여 필수적인 영어 커뮤니케이션 능력을 갖추고 향상시키는 것을 목적으로 씌어졌다.

13개의 Unit로 구성되어 있고, 탑승부터 시작하여 좌석, 기내 서비스, 이륙에 이르기까지 여러 가지 기내에서 일어날 수 있는 다양한 상황 속에서 승무원들이 꼭 알아야 하는 항공영어 어휘, 표현, 회화들을 체계적으로 정리하여 수록하였다. 각 Unit는 Vocabulary and Useful Expressions, Dialogues, Say It In English, Reading, Activities 순서의 구조를 가지고 있다. Say It In English는 Useful Expressions를 반복 훈련하여 표현들을 자연스럽게 정리 할 수 있게 되어있는 장치이고, Activities는 Vocabulary, Dialogues들을 반복하여 정리하기 위함이다.

이 책을 공부하는 모든 사람들이 쉽고, 재미있게 flight attendant 영어 실력이 강화되고, 직무를 수행하는데 있어 자신감을 갖게 되리라 확신하면서 이 책이 출판되도록 수고해 주신, 최은아 선생님, 백산출판사 진욱상 사장님과 편집부 여러분께 감사를 드립니다.

2007. 1. 김 현 수

Introduction

This book has been designed to help those who want to be flight attendants to use English for communicating with passengers in many different situations. The units have been organized beginning with situations of first contact with passengers and progressing sequentially throughout the possible communication requirements during a typical flight.

The units have been divided into five parts. Each unit opens with a list of vocabulary and useful expressions to introduce terminology that will be required throughout that unit. Following the vocabulary, dialogues make up the main part of each unit. The dialogues are intended to assist students in formulating conversations of their own by providing the necessary base of conversation for most situations they will encounter on the aircraft. The Say It In English sections will help to reinforce what students have learned in the Useful Expressions by checking their ability to translate the Korean phrase or sentence into English. The reading section that follows will test students' comprehension of the sections they have already learned and introduce new material to supplement the unit. Finally, the activities at the end of each unit will give students practice using and recognizing what they have learned. There is also an appendix section that provides additional activities, should they want extra practice.

We sincerely hope that you and the students enjoy the material and learn a lot from it. With this text as a base and their own practice and confidence, we are sure that students will be able to communicate well in the situations they will face in their jobs as flight attendants.

2007. 1. Reashelle Braiden

CONTENTS

Unit 1

1 BOARDING

Vocabulary and Useful expressions

steward(ess) passenger aisle

boarding pass cabin business class

tour conductor upstairs

- Welcome aboard.
- May I see your boarding pass, please?
- Where is my seat?
- Take the aisle to your right.
- Your seat is in the front of the cabin.
- Have a nice flight.

Dialogues

C : Cabin crew P : Passenger

Dialogue 1

C : Good morning. Welcome aboard. May I see your boarding pass, please?

P : Here it is. Where is my seat?

C : Your seat number is 35A. Please take the aisle to your right.

P : Thank you.

C : You're welcome. Have a nice flight.

Dialogue 2

C : Good afternoon. May I see your boarding pass, please?

P : Yes, here you are.

C : 20H. It's over there. Your seat is in the front of the cabin, on your left. It's an aisle seat.

P : Thanks a lot.

C : My pleasure. Have a good flight.

Dialogue 3

C : Good evening, sir. Welcome aboard. May I see your boarding pass?

P : Just a moment. Here it is.

C : Your seat number is 40B. Please take this aisle. Your seat is at the back of the cabin, on your right. It's a window seat.

P : Thank you very much.

C : You're welcome.

Dialogue 4

C : Good afternoon, ma'am. Welcome aboard. Do you know your seat number?

P : It's 7-A.

C : Business class is upstairs. Please use those stairs.

P : Thank you.

C : You're welcome. Enjoy your flight, ma'am.

Dialogue 5

C : Good morning, sir. Welcome aboard.

P : I'm a tour conductor with the Jangan Tour Company.

C : How many people do you have in your party?

P : We are fifteen, including myself.

C : Alright, sir. I'll show you to your seat. Come this way, please.

P : Thank you. Would you show my guests to their seats?

C : Of course.

If you are interested in Aircraft Type and Seat Position, please refer to the appendix.

Say it in English

1. (우리비행기에) 탑승 하신 것을 환영합니다.

2. 탑승권 좀 보여 주시겠습니까?

3. 오른쪽 통로로 가세요.

4. 손님 좌석은 기내 뒤쪽입니다.

5. 즐거운 비행되시길 바랍니다.

Reading

Announcement:

"Ladies and gentlemen, we wish to welcome you aboard North West Airlines Flight 203. This flight is bound for Chicago. The captain of this flight is Donald King. Today's flight time will be 12 hours. Our captain will provide you with more flight information after take-off. For your comfort and safety there are 12 flight attendants on board today. If there is anything we can do for you, please let us know. We wish you a pleasant flight. Thank you."

Answer the following questions.

1. What is the captain's name?

2. What is the flight number?

3. Where is this flight bound for?

4. How long is the flight time?

5. How many flight attendants are on board?

Activities

A. Unscramble the tiles below to reveal a message.

1.

wel	a	co	board	me

2.

pa	ing	bo	ss	ard

3.

ere	Wh	se	my	is	at	?

4.

isle	ke	Ta	the	a

5.

ght	ce	in	Ha	fli	ve	a

B. Match each question with the appropriate response.

1) May I see your boarding pass, please?

2) How many people do you have in your party?

3) Where is my seat?

4) Would you show my guests to their seats?

5) I'll show you to your seats. Come this way, please.

_____ a) We are fifteen, including myself.

_____ b) Thank you.

_____ c) Your seat numbers is 35A.

_____ d) Here it is.

_____ e) Of course.

C. Search for the words below in the puzzle.

c	p	a	s	s	e	n	g	e	r
o	a	i	b	a	b	o	a	r	d
n	c	s	d	e	f	k	m	u	n
d	g	l	h	i	j	l	s	p	o
u	w	e	l	c	o	m	e	s	t
c	p	v	w	a	x	y	a	t	u
t	q	a	t	b	a	n	t	a	n
o	r	b	o	i	c	e	o	i	g
r	s	e	u	n	o	m	c	r	e
s	t	e	w	a	r	d	e	s	s

passenger	cabin	seat
aisle	stewardess	boarding
conductor	welcome	upstairs

If you need more activities, please refer to the appendix.

Unit 2

2 IN THE CABIN

Vocabulary and Useful expressions

compartment	overhead	underneath
cooperation	rack	in front of

- May I help you with your bags?
- Are these all your bags?
- I will put them in the overhead compartment.
- Where can I put my bag?
- You can put it underneath the seat.

Dialogues

C : Cabin crew　　P : Passenger

Dialogue 1

C : Good morning. May I help you with your bags, ma'am?

P : Yes, please. Thank you.

C : You're welcome. Are these all your bags?

P : Yes, they are.

C : I will put them in the overhead compartment.

P : Thank you very much.

C : You're welcome.

Dialogue 2

C : Good afternoon. May I help you?

P : Miss, where can I put my bag?

C : You can put it underneath the seat in front of you or in the overhead compartment.

P : Thank you.

C : Not at all.

Dialogue 3

C : Are these your bags?

P : Yes, they are.

C : Why don't you put them underneath your seat, if you don't mind?

P : Alright. I'll do that.

C : Thank you for your cooperation.

P : You're welcome.

C : If you need anything during the flight, please let us know.

P : It's very kind of you. Thanks.

Dialogue 4

C : Good morning. May I help you?

P : Yes, where can I put my bag?

C : You can put it here, at your feet.

P : Thanks. What about my coat and hat?

C : You can put your coat and small items on the rack overhead.

P : Thank you.

C : You're welcome.

Say it in English

1. 당신 가방을 좀 들어드릴까요?

2. 이것들이 당신 가방들 입니까?

3. 당신 머리위에 짐 넣어두는 장에 그 가방을 넣어드리겠습니다.

4. 내 가방을 어디다 두지요?

5. 당신 발밑에 두세요.

Reading

History of the Airplane

The dream of flying is as old as mankind itself. However, the concept of the airplane has only been around for two centuries. Before that time, men and women tried to navigate the air by imitating the birds.[1)]

The first successful flight of a powered airplane occurred in North Carolina, U.S,A., on December 17, 1903. The airplane's designers were Orville and Wilbur Wright. The first plane was very primitive, but within a few years, aircraft designers, had made many improvements. The first flight only lasted twelve seconds and traveled 120 feet, but a later flight that day lasted fifty-nine seconds and traveled 852 feet.

Airplanes were first used for military purposes during World War I, but only in very limited ways. After World War I, there were additional advances in airplane design that made flights much safer. Later, planes would be used for military, commercial, and passenger transportation purposes.[2)]

1) source: www.first-to-fly.com
2) source: www.ohiohistorycentral.org

Answer the following questions.

1. Who were the first designers of the plane?

2. How long did the first flight last?

3. For what purposes were airplanes first used?

4. For what purposes were airplanes later used?

Activities

A. In the box below you'll find a number of chopped words. Find the pieces that fit together and write the words in the space provided below.

ment	com	der
over	neath	tion
un	opera	he
co	n	part
bi	ca	ad

Write the correct words below.

1. ______________________

2. ______________________

3. ______________________

4. ______________________

5. ______________________

B. Please fill in the blanks with the proper words below.

seat	put	overhead	help	bags

1. May I ____________ you with your bags?
2. Where can I ________________ my bags?
3. You can ______________ it underneath the ______________ .
4. Are these your ______________? Yes, they are.
5. I will put them in the __________________ compartment.

Unit 3

3 SEATING

Vocabulary and Useful expressions

assign

separate

occupied

window seat

aisle seat

inconvenience

non-smoking zone

We want to sit together. Is that possible?

I'll see if it can be arranged, sir.

I'm sorry, but all seats are occupied.

Excuse me, may I change seats?

We have lots of empty seats at the back.

Where would you like to sit?

I'm sorry for the inconvenience, sir.

Dialogues

C : Cabin crew   P : Passenger 1

Dialogue 1

P : Excuse me, my friend and I are sitting in separate seats. Is it possible for us to sit together?

C : Yes, ma'am. We have some empty seats in the back of the cabin. Would that be alright, sir?

P : That would be fine.

C : This way, please.

(......)

C : Here you are. Have a nice flight, sir.

P : Thank you.

Dialogue 2

P1 : Excuse me, my wife is sitting over there and we want to sit together. Is that possible?

C : I'll see if it can be arranged, sir.
After take-off, I'll come back and let you know.

(......)

C : I'm sorry, sir, but all the seats are occupied. Where is your wife sitting?

P1: Just across the aisle over there.

C : Just a moment, please.

(Goes to P2 to ask about changing seats)

C : Excuse me, sir. I'm sorry to bother you. We have a couple who has been assigned separate seats. Would you mind changing seats so they can sit together?

P2: No, I don't. Where should I sit?

C : Thank you very much, sir. This way please.

(......)

C : I'm sorry for the inconvenience, sir. Would you care for something to drink?

P2: No, thank you.

C : This gentleman is willing to change seats with you. This way, please.

(......)

C : Here you are.

P1: Thank you. I appreciate it.

C : My pleasure. Have a nice flight.

Dialogue 3

P : Excuse me, may I change seats?

C : Yes, you may. We have lots of empty seats at the back. Where would you like to sit?

P : I'd like a window seat.

C : Please come this way, sir.

P : Thank you.

C : You're welcome.

Dialogue 4

P : Do you have empty seats in the front of the cabin?

C : Just a moment, please. I'll see if there are empty seats in the front.

(......)

C : We have empty seats in the middle of the cabin. Would that be alright, sir?

P : Yes, that'll be fine.

C : This way, please.

C : Here you are. Have a nice flight.

Dialogue 5

P : Excuse me, I want to change seats.

C : Where would you like to sit, sir?

P : In the front, if possible.

C : I'll see if it can be arranged.

(......)

C : Thank you for waiting. I'm sorry, but I'm afraid all the seats in the front are occupied. Would you care for something to drink?

P : No, thank you.

C : If you need anything during the flight, please let me know.

Dialogue 6

P : Excuse me. Something's wrong here. We both have the same seat number.

S : May I see your boarding pass, please? Thank you. I'm sorry sir. There has been a mistake with the seating arrangement. Would you mind waiting while I check on this?

(······)

S : Thank you for waiting, sir. I have a seat for you. Your seat number is 25-B.

It's an aisle seat. Please follow me. I'm sorry for the inconvenience.

P : That's alright.

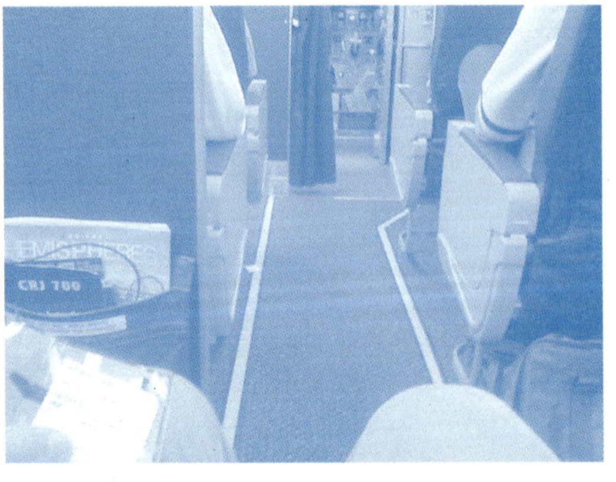

Say it in English

1. 우리는 함께 앉기를 원합니다.

2. 뒤쪽에 빈자리가 많이 있습니다.

3. 죄송하지만 좌석을 바꿀 수 있나요?

4. 어디에 앉기를 원하십니까?

5. 불편을 끼쳐드려 죄송합니다.

Reading

Jie-soo and Eun-Hee are flight attendants. They work for North West Airlines. They fly from Seoul to Chicago and back every week. They enjoy their work very much and take good care of their passengers. They meet them at the door and give each passenger a lot of attention. They make them comfortable. During the flight their passengers eat delicious food. They listen to music and watch movies and they also read magazines. The passengers like Jie-soo and Eun-Hee. They're pleasant and sociable. They always smile.

Answer the following questions.

1. Which airline do they work for?

2. What do they do?

3. Where do they fly every week?

4. Who makes the passengers comfortable?

5. Why do the passengers like Jie-soo and Eun-Hee?

Activities

A. Match the first part of the conversation on the left with the correct response from the list on the right.

1. Excuse me, may I change seats?	a. No, we don't. But we have empty seats in the middle of the cabin.
2. We want to sit together. Is that possible?	b. Yes, you may. We have lots of empty seats.
3. Do you have empty seats in the front of the cabin?	c. No, I don't. Where should I sit?
4. Would you mind changing seats with me?	d. I'll see if it can be arranged, sir.

B. It's a Bingo game. Say Bingo when your sheet is ready.

assign	inconvenience	occupy
window seat	change	aisle seat
front	middle	back

change	window seat	front	non-smoking
middle	occupy	assign	separate
inconvenience	back	aisle seat	together

Free Bingo Space

Unit 4

4 PREPARATION FOR TAKE-OFF

Vocabulary and Useful expressions

fasten	insert	buckle
take-off	upright	regulation
safety	tray	put out
turn off	magazine	

- Would you mind fastening your seat belt, please?
- Could you please put out your cigarette?
- Smoking is not allowed on the aircraft.
- Would you mind closing your tray table, please?
- Would you put your seat in the upright position, please?
- We'll be taking off soon.
- Would you like a newspaper or a magazine?

Dialogues

C : Cabin crew　　P : Passenger

Dialogue 1

C : Would you mind fastening your seat belt, please? We'll be taking off soon.

P : Oh, sure. (Fastens the seat belt)

C : Would you put your seat in the upright position, please?

P : Is this alright?

C : Yes, thank you.

P : You're welcome.

Dialogue 2

C : Please fasten your seat belt.

P : Will you show me how to fasten my seat belt?

C : Of course. Pull it this way and just insert this part of the belt into this buckle.

P : Oh, I see. Thanks.

C : You're welcome. If you need any help, just push this call button.

Dialogue 3

C : Excuse me, sir. Would you mind fastening your seat belt, please?

P : I don't like fastening my seat belt. Don't worry. Nothing will happen.

C : I'm sorry, but I must ask you to fasten it for take-off. We can not depart until all passengers have fastened their seat belts. It's also for your own safety, sir.

P : Alright.

C : Thank you for your cooperation. You can unfasten your seat belt when the captain turns off the seat belt sign following take-off.

P : Oh, I see. Thanks.

C : You're welcome.

Dialogue 4

C : Excuse me, ma'am. Would you mind closing your tray table, please?

P : O.K.

C : Thank you, ma'am. You may use it again following take-off.

P : Alright.

C : Could you please put out your cigarette? Smoking is not allowed on the aircraft.

P : I'm sorry.

C : That's alright, ma'am. We'll be taking off shortly. Have a nice flight.

Dialogue 5

C : Would you like to read a newspaper, sir?

P : Oh, yes. Could I have the Dong-A daily?

C : Yes, here you are.

P : Thank you.

C : You're welcome.

Dialogue 6

C : Excuse me, sir. Would you like a newspaper or a magazine ?

P : Yes. Do you have the Chicago Times?

C : I'm sorry, sir. We have run out. Would you care for the New York Times, instead?

P : Oh, that's fine.

C : Here you are. Have a pleasant flight.

Say it in English

1. 안전벨트를 매 주시겠습니까?

2. 우리는 곧 이륙할 것입니다.

3. 담배를 꺼 주시겠습니까?

4. 좌석 등받이를 세워 주시겠습니까?

5. 신문이나 잡지를 보시겠습니까?

Reading

Announcements :

1. "Ladies and gentlemen, we will be taking off shortly. Please make sure that your seat back is in the upright position, your tray table is closed and your seat belt is fastened. We recommend that you keep your seat belt fastened while seated during the flight. Also, refrain from using any electronic devices during take–off and landing for safety reasons. Your cooperation will be much appreciated. If there is anything we can do for you, please let us know. We wish you a pleasant flight. Thank you."

2. "Ladies and gentlemen, because of the current weather conditions at Incheon Airport, our departure is going to be delayed about twenty minutes. We'll take off as soon as possible. Thank you."

3. "Ladies and gentlemen, the weather conditions at Incheon Airport have not improved yet. Unfortunately, we must remain here until weather conditions improve. We will make another announcement following the nine o'clock weather report. Thank you for your understanding and patience. We apologize for the delay."

Before departure, we have to follow some safety procedures. Put a check(V) in front of the statements that tell us what we have to do.

( ) 1. We have to make sure that our seat is in the upright position.

( ) 2. We have to read a newspaper or a magazine.

( ) 3. We have to close our tray table.

( ) 4. We have to go to the bathroom before take-off.

( ) 5. We have to fasten our seat belts.

Answer the following questions about the reading.

1. Why is the airplane going to be delayed?

2. How long will it be delayed?

3. Where is this flight going to take off from?

Activities

A. Please fill in the blanks with the proper words in the box.

off	upright	fastening	closing	put

1. Would you mind ____________ your seat belt, please?
2. We will be taking ___________ soon.
3. Could you please ____________ out your cigarette?
4. Would you put your seat in the ____________ position, please?
5. Would you mind __________ your tray table, please?

B. Find the pieces that fit together among the chopped words below, and write the words on the space provided below.

in	co	right
fast	sert	en
up	reg	opera
ula	tion	tion

Write the correct words below.

1. ______________

2. ______________

3. ______________

4. ______________

5. ______________

Unit 5

5 EN-ROUTE

Vocabulary and Useful expressions

aisle	window	seatbelt
tray table	fasten	in-flight magazine
non-smoking	upright	seat pocket

- Excuse me, miss?
- Please fasten your seatbelt.
- Please return your seat to its upright position.
- The entire flight is non-smoking.
- Refer to your in-flight magazine.
- Is there a problem?
- Thank you for your cooperation.

Dialogues

C : Cabin crew　　P : Passenger

Dialogue 1

C : Please fasten your seatbelt, ma'am.

P : I am going to talk to my friend a few rows up. I won't be long.

C : I'm sorry ma'am. The captain has turned on the fasten seat belt light.

P : Is there a problem?

C : No, we are just expecting some turbulence. It's for your safety.

P : Well, thank you. I'll just wait.

C : Thank you for your cooperation.

Dialogue 2

P : Is there anywhere I can smoke on this plane?

C : No. I'm sorry sir. The entire flight is non-smoking.

P : Is that for every flight?

C : Yes, sir. It is a law. All flights are now non-smoking.

P : How long before we land?

C : Approximately one hour. Sorry, you will have to wait until then.

P : Yes, I will. Thanks.

Dialogue 3

P : Excuse me, miss?

C : Yes, maam?

P : My carry-on bags are in the overhead compartment about four rows up. Is it alright to get them now?

C : The captain has just turned off the seatbelt sign. It should be fine but please fasten your seatbelt when you return to your seat. Do you need any help?

P : No, that's alright. Thank you.

C : Can I help you with anything else?

P : No, that's fine.

Say it in English

1. 실례합니다.

2. 비행중에는 금연입니다.

3. 기내잡지를 참고해 주십시오.

4. 무슨 문제가 있습니까?

5. 협조해 주셔서 감사합니다.

Reading

Captain's In-Flight Announcement:

"Good afternoon passengers. This is your captain speaking. I hope you are enjoying your flight so far. We are now flying at an altitude of 9000 meters and at an airspeed of 650 kilometers per hour. The current time is 1:25 pm. We expect to arrive in Vancouver on schedule at 9:45. The weather at our destination is cool and sunny, with a high of 15 degrees celcius. The cabin crew will be around in about ten minutes to offer you a light snack and beverage, and the in-flight movie will begin soon after that. Relax and enjoy the rest of the flight."

Answer the following questions.

1. How quickly are they going?

2. What is the arrival time?

3. How high is the plane flying?

4. When will the cabin crew come around?

5. Where are they going?

6. How's the weather at their destination?

Activities

A. Fill in the blanks using the picture below.

1. There is nobody in the seat ________ me.
2. The bag is ___________ the seat.
3. The overhead bin is ________ the seat.
4. The passenger _______ me is kicking my seat.
5. The cup is _____ the tray table.
6. The man _________ of me has his seat too far back.

B. You will often have to use a 24-hour clock when discussing flight times. Below is a list of the 24-hour clock times. Review them and practice with the clocks on the right.

12–hour clock	24–hour clock
12:00 am (midnight)	00:00
1:00 am	1:00
2:00 am	2:00
3:00 am	3:00
4:00 am	4:00
5:00 am	5:00
6:00 am	6:00
7:00 am	7:00
8:00 am	8:00
9:00 am	9:00
10:00 am	10:00
11:00 am	11:00
12:00 pm (noon)	12:00
1:00 pm	13:00
2:00 pm	14:00
3:00 pm	15:00
4:00 pm	16:00
5:00 pm	17:00
6:00 pm	18:00
7:00 pm	19:00
8:00 pm	20:00
9:00 pm	21:00
10:00 pm	22:00
11:00 pm	23:00

Write the 24–hour clock time under the clocks below.

11:15 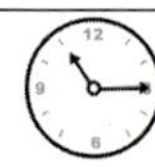	1:50 
8:30 	6:20 
9:45 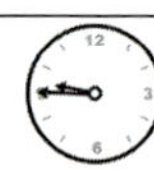	1:30 
4:40 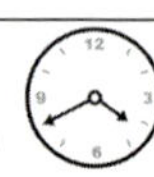	3:25 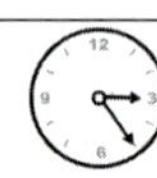
10:10 	12:05 

C. Speaking Activity- Stand Up!

Walk around the room and interview your classmates. Don't stop until you have had each question answered by a different classmate. Try to put their responses into new sentences. The first one is done for you. Now, find someone….

who has studied English before.
(Have you studied English before?)
James has studied English before.

who has never been on an airplane.
(Have you been on an airplane?)
____

who prefers an aisle seat to a window seat.
____

who wants to travel to Africa.
____

who has never been outside of Korea.
____

who can speak three languages.
____

who can sleep easily during a flight.
____

who has been to an English speaking country.
____

who doesn't like spicy food.
____

who enjoys scary movies.
____

D. Now write sentences about yourself.

1. I have studied English for two years.

2.

3.

4.

5.

6.

7.

8.

9.

10.

If you need more activities, please refer to the appendix.

Unit 6

IN-FLIGHT SERVICE AND SALES

Vocabulary and Useful expressions

refreshments, beverage, allergy

vegetarian, duty-free, headset

blanket, complimentary, pillow

- What would you like? The chicken or fish?
- Enjoy your meal.
- Could I please have a blanket?
- How do I order this perfume?
- Can I pay in US dollars?
- Would you like some headphones?
- Which English movies will be showing?

Dialogues

C : Cabin crew **P** : Passenger

Food Service

Dialogue 1

C : I will be coming around with the meal cart for dinner in a moment.

P : Great! I am getting hungry.

C : Here we are. What would you like? The chicken or fish?

P : I'll have chicken. What kind of vegetables does it come with?

C : Carrots and onions, sir.

P : Sure. That's fine. Thank you.

C : Would you like a roll with your meal?

P : Oh, no thank you, but I would like more salt and pepper.

C : Here you are. Enjoy your meal.

P : Thanks.

Dialogue 2

C : Good morning, sir. Would you like the breakfast omelet or the bibimbap?

P : What is bibimbap?

C : It's a Korean dish. It's mixed rice with vegetables, beef and a spicy sauce called gochujang.

P : Sounds good, but I don't eat beef. I'll have the breakfast omelet.

C : Are you a vegetarian? The omelet comes with bacon.

P : No, I'm not. I don't eat beef but pork is fine.

C : Alright, sir. Here is your omelet. Can I get you anything else?

P : Yes, I'll have some orange juice, please.

C : Here you are. Enjoy.

P : Thanks!

□ Blanket and Pillow Service

Dialogue 3

P : Excuse me. Could I please have a blanket? I'm really cold.

C : Of course ma'am. I will get you one right away.

P : Oh, could I also have a pillow?

C : Sure, I will be right back.

P : Thanks.

(......)

C : Here you go. Would you like anything else?

P : No, this is fine. Thank you very much.

C : You're welcome. Just press the call-button if you need anything.

□ Duty-Free Sales

Dialogue 4

P : Excuse me. Can you tell me where to find the duty-free items sales?

C : Sure. The duty-free catalogue is in the seat pocket in front of you.

P : Great! Thank you. Can you help me?

C : Sure. These are the items that we have available for sale. The prices are under the photo.

P : How do I order this perfume?

C : Here is the form. Just fill it out and we will put the order together for you. Would you like to pay by credit card or cash?

P : Can I pay in U.S. dollars or do you need Korean won?

C : Either is fine, sir.

P : I'll pay in US dollars. Thanks for your help.

C : You're welcome. No problem at all.

□ Movie and music service

Dialogue 5

C : Sir, the in-flight movie will be beginning soon. Would you like some headphones?

P : Yes, thank you. Which English movies will be showing?

C : There are quite a few. You can look at the schedule in the in-flight magazine. Here it is in the seat pocket.

P : Oh great. What page are the movies on?

C : For this flight, they are on page 27.

P : Thank you. I'll have a look.

C : You're welcome. Your English station is channel 1.
Let me know if you need anything else.

P : I will. Thanks very much.

Dialogue 6

C : For your comfort on this flight bound for Tokyo, we are happy to provide a wide selection of music and talk radio.

P : I am looking for a classical music station and I can't seem to find one.

C : We have two classical stations. One is channel 11 and the other is channel 6.

P : Well, thank you. I don't know how I missed them.
Is there a listing of your stations?

C : Yes. Your in-flight magazine has the list of channels on page 24.

P : Thanks. That's very helpful.

C : You're welcome.

Say it in English

1. 무엇을 드시겠습니까?

2. 맛있게 드세요.

3. 담요 한 장 주시겠어요?

4. 이 향수를 어떻게 주문하지요?

5. 어떤 영화가 상영됩니까?

Reading

In-flight Service Announcement :

"Ladies and gentlemen, this is your head flight attendant, Steve Kim. I hope you are enjoying your flight. In a few minutes, we'll be serving cocktails and soft drinks, followed by lunch. Duty-free sales will follow the meal service. Today, we have two movies for your entertainment. Two hours before arrival, a snack will be served. For further details on service during the flight, please refer to your in-flight magazine. We wish you a pleasant flight. Thank you."

Meal Service Announcement :

"Good afternoon ladies and gentlemen. I hope you are enjoying the flight. The flight attendants are now coming around with the beverage and snack cart. In about 15 minutes, we will be interrupting the movie briefly to serve dinner. The choices for today are chicken with rice and vegetables and beef with noodles. I hope that you are enjoying the movie. If you have any questions, or you need anything, please let one of our cabin crew know."

Answer the following questions.

1. What are they serving for dinner?

2. When will they be serving dinner?

3. What are the flight attendants doing during this announcement?

4. Is this the beginning, middle or end of the flight?

Activities

A. Write the name of each of the items below in the spaces.

a) Put a circle around each item that you drink.

b) Put a square around each item that you eat.

c) Put a triangle around each item that you can use to eat.

d) Put a line through each item that you can put in food.

e) Put a line under each item that you use to sleep

beer

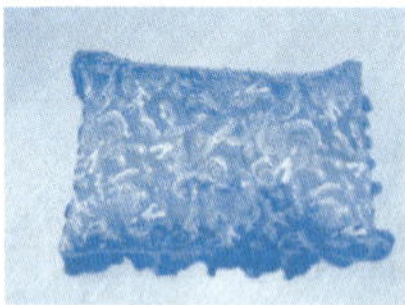
pillow

blanket

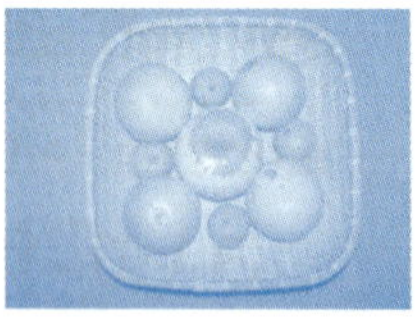
fruit

meat

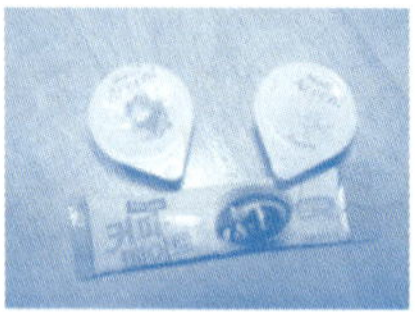
cream

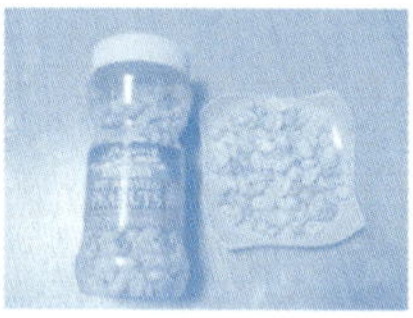
nuts

juice

salt

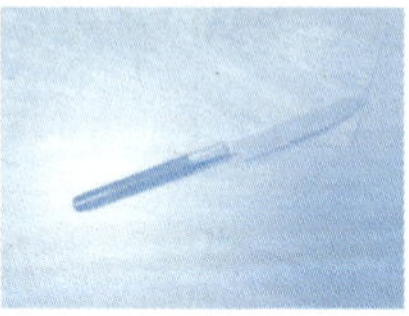
knife

spoon

vegetables

tea

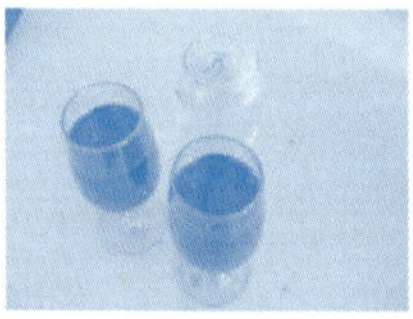
wine

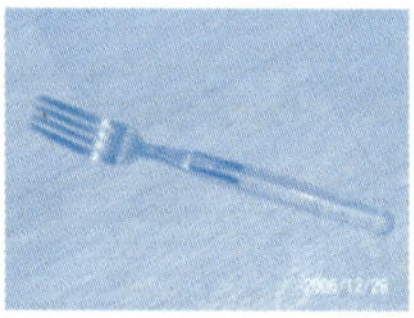
fork

pepper

coffee

chopsticks

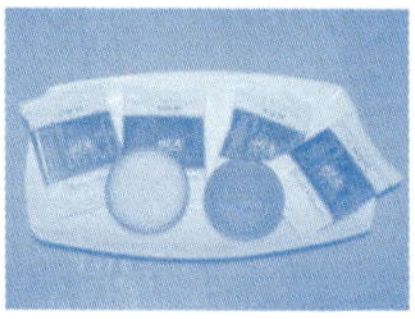
cookies

sugar

B. Put the vocabulary words into Korean and then use them in an English sentence.

	Korean	Use it in a sentence.
duty-free	______	______
vegetarian	______	______
complimentary	______	______
refreshments	______	______
headset	______	______
channel	______	______
beverage	______	______
blanket	______	______
pillow	______	______
allergy	______	______

C. Fill in the blanks with the words from the list below.

tea	sprite	juice	coffee
milk	coke	spirits	wine
beer	nuts	vegetables	fruit
meat	cookies	roll(bun)	sugar
cream	fork	spoon	knife
chopsticks	salt	pepper	fanta

1. I'd like some _____ and _______ for my coffee, please.
2. We have orange _________ and green _____.
3. In our bar cart we have _______, red and white ______ and many different types of __________.
4. I'm a vegetarian, I don't eat ___________.
5. Can I have a snack, please? Maybe some chocolate chip _______ or some mixed ______.
6. My ______ fell on the floor. I can't cut my chicken.
7. I don't know how to use these ____________. Can I have a fork, please.
8. Can I please have some _________ and _________ to add flavor to my meal?
9. Would you please give me another _______ to stir my drink?
10. What kind of ____________ are in the omelette? I don't like onions or carrots.
11. Do you have any __________? I really would like an apple.
12. We have three kinds of soda pop. _________, _________ and ________.

D. Match the answer from the following questions. The first one is done for you.

1. When will we be eating?
2. Do you serve tomato juice?
3. Where are my headphones?
4. Can I please have some more coffee?
5. Where do I find the movie listing?
6. How do I change the music?
7. When will I get my duty-free purchases?
8. How much is the total?
9. Is there more than one Korean movie playing?
10. Can you take my tray? I'm finished.

___ a) No, I'm sorry. We don't.

___ b) Of course, would you like cream and sugar?

___ c) It'll be $294.50

_1_ d) In another 30 minutes.

___ e) Just press this button to change the channels.

___ f) Sure. There are three.

___ g) Yes, no problem.

___ h) Here they are.

___ i) We will bring it around once it is prepared.

___ j) It's in the seat pocket in front of you.

If you need more activities, please refer to the appendix.

Unit 7

7 SPECIAL PROBLEMS WITH PASSENGERS

Vocabulary and Useful expressions

airsickness	indigestion	allergy
first aid	sore throat	headache
burned	disturbing	cold

- I think I'm going to throw up.
- Do you have any medicine for airsickness?
- Do you have any allergies?
- Please calm down.
- If you take full responsibility, we may give you first aid medication.
- Have you tried it before?
- I hope you feel better.

Dialogues

C : Cabin crew P : Passenger

Dialogue 1

C : Excuse me, miss, are you alright?

P : No, I don't think so. I think I'm going to throw up.

C : Here is an airsickness bag. Can I help you to the bathroom?

P : Yes, please. Thank you. Do you have any medicine for airsickness?

C : Yes, we do. I'll get some for you. Have you taken airsickness medication before?

P : Yes, I have. Could I also have some water?

C : Sure, one moment, please.

Dialogue 2

C : Excuse me, ma'am. Please put out your cigarette and come out of the bathroom.

P : What is the problem?

C : Ma'am, by aviation law, smoking is not allowed on any aircraft.

P : I was in the bathroom. I wasn't bothering anyone.

C : I have to inform you that smoking is against the law and will be reported to the captain and the airport police.

P : OK, I'm sorry, don't do that. I will return to my seat.

C : Thank you for your cooperation.

Dialogue 3

P : Excuse me, miss? I need another vodka.

C : I'm very sorry sir, but I can not serve you any more alcohol. You have already had four and are disturbing other passengers. Remember, alcohol affects you more at high altitudes.

P : I know that. I am not disturbing anyone. I am being very quiet!

C : I have already had some complaints. Please calm down. I can get you a soda, if you'd like.

P : No thanks. I said I want vodka!

C : Well, sir, if you continue to disrupt the other passengers, we will have to report you to the airport police.

P : OK, OK. Please just get me a Sprite.

Dialogue 4

P : Excuse me, miss. I have a headache. Do you have any medicine for that?

C : I'm sorry to hear that. We have Tylenol for headaches. Do you have any allergies?

P : No, I don't.

C : If you take full responsibility, we may give you first aid medication. Have you tried it before?

P : Yes, please can I have <u>a Tylenol</u> and water?

C : I'll bring you some right away.

P : Thanks very much.

C : You're welcome. I hope you feel better.

Say it in English

1. 멀미약 있습니까?

2. 이전에 이약을 드신 적이 있으십니까?

3. 엘러지가 있으신지요?

4. 좀 나아지시길 바랍니다.

Reading

Mr. Jones booked airplane tickets for himself, his wife and their three-year old son departing from Seoul and arriving in Vancouver, Canada. At the time of booking, he reserved a window seat and the two seats next to it. He also requested a vegetarian meal for himself and a kosher meal for his wife. When Mr. Jones and his family arrived at the airport, they were given boarding passes, they checked in and boarded the plane. When they got on the plane, he realized that they had seats in the center aisle. After this problem was taken care of by the flight attendant, the family was happy until it was meal time and there were no vegetarian meals left!

Answer the following questions.

1. Where is the Jones family going?

2. How many seats did they book?

3. What kind of meal does Mr. Jones' wife want?

4. What would you say to Mr. Jones when he complains about the wrong seating?

5. How would you explain the missing vegetarian meal?

Activities

A. Work with a partner and fill in the blanks with medicine you can take for each of the problems. Substitute the underlined parts in Dialogue 4 with the words and phrases below and try the conversation again.

a cold	________________
indigestion	________________
a sore throat	________________
a burn	ointment for a burn
allergies	________________

B. Answer the questions with a partner.

a) Name three illnesses passengers may complain about on an airplane.

________________, ________________, ________________.

b) Name three things you can give someone if they are sick.

________________, ________________, ________________.

c) Name three things that are against the law on an airplane.

________________, ________________, ________________.

d) Name three things the flight attendant should do if a passenger is disturbing other passengers.

________________, ________________, ________________.

C. Unscramble each of the clue words. Copy the letters in the numbered cells to the cells below with the same number.

Clue	Cells
NIIKESCARSS	☐☐☐☐☐☐☐☐☐(2)☐☐
HEDCEAHA	☐☐☐☐☐☐☐☐(6)
DIMIEECN	☐☐☐☐(4)☐☐☐☐
GERLALY	☐☐(3)☐☐☐☐☐
NAIGTSA TEH AWL	☐☐☐☐☐☐☐(5) ☐☐☐ ☐☐☐
SRTIF IAD	☐☐☐☐☐ ☐☐☐
TUSDIRGINB	☐☐☐☐☐☐☐(1)☐☐☐

☐	☐		p	o	☐	☐	☐	☐
1	2				3	4	5	6

D. Vocabulary Practice

	Korean	Use it in a sentence.
airsickness	________	____________________
first aid	________	____________________
burned	________	____________________
indigestion	________	____________________
sore throat	________	____________________
allergy	________	____________________
headache	________	____________________
cold	________	____________________
disturbing	________	____________________

Unit 8

EMERGENCY SITUATIONS

Vocabulary and Useful expressions

life jacket | oxygen mask | turbulence
evacuation | emergency exit | instructions
immediately

- You must return to your seat immediately.
- We are experiencing some turbulence.
- Just remain seated, please.
- It's an emergency.
- Is there a doctor on board?
- What is the problem?
- This passenger is very ill. Can you take a look at him?

Dialogues

C : Cabin crew **P** : Passenger

Dialogue 1

C : Excuse me sir. You must return to your seat immediately.

P : Why? What's wrong?

C : The captain has turned on the seatbelt sign. We are experiencing some turbulence.

P : How long will it last?

C : It shouldn't be too long, maybe 5 or 10 minutes.

P : OK, thanks. I hope it's not too bad.

C : I don't think it will be. Just remain seated and it should be fine.

Dialogue 2

C : Excuse me passengers, is there a doctor on board? It's an emergency.

P : I am a doctor. What is the problem?

C : This passenger is very ill. Can you take a look at him?

P : Sure. Let's go find out what is wrong with him.

C : Thank you for your help.

P : You're welcome.

Dialogue 3

C : Good afternoon sir. Welcome aboard. You are sitting at the emergency exit. Are you willing to help us with an evacuation, if necessary?

P : Sure, but what do I have to do?

C : You would help the cabin crew to evacuate the airplane but please do not open the exit door without instructions from us.

P : Alright, is there anything else?

C : Yes, please read this briefing card over and let me know if you have any questions.

P : Thank you. I will.

Say it in English

1. 기내에 의사선생님 계십니까?

2. 무슨 일이지요?

3. 응급상황이 발생했습니다.

4. 자리에 앉아 있어주세요.

5. 이 승객이 대단히 아픕니다. 좀 봐주시겠어요?

Reading

Announcement:

"Attention passengers. This is your captain speaking. As you see, I have turned on the seat belt sign. We are experiencing some severe turbulence. Please return to your seats immediately and fasten your seat belts. Food and beverage service will be suspended until we are through the worst of it. Although we do not expect it to last long, it may be a very bumpy ride for a few minutes. Please remain in your seats with your seat belts fastened and refrain from getting up to use the lavatory until I turn off the seat belt sign. Thank you very much for your cooperation."

Answer the following questions.

1. Why must passengers return to their seats?

2. Will they continue serving food and drinks?

3. Will the turbulence last long?

4. Can passengers go to the bathroom during the turbulence?

5. How long does the captain expect the turbulence to last?

Activities

A. Unscramble the tiles below to reveal a message.

1.

ca	st	lm	ase	ple	ay

2.

have	gency	an	we	emer

3.

oxy	ma	gen	sk

4.

it	ex	em	gency	er

5.

seat	main	ed	re

B. Vocabulary Practice

	Korean	Use it in a sentence
life jacket	___________	_____________________________
oxygen mask	___________	_____________________________
turbulence	___________	_____________________________
emergency exit	___________	_____________________________
instructions	___________	_____________________________
immediately	___________	_____________________________

C. Put the sentences in the correct Subject-Verb-Object order and then in each corrected sentence, put a circle around the subject, underline the verb and put a triangle around the object. Your sentences should be marked as follows.

Example : eat dinner I 10p.m. at. ○ I <u>eat</u> △ dinner at 10 p.m.

a) going is the He to bathroom. ______________________

b) served Dinner being is. ______________________

c) fasten belt Please seat your. ______________________

d) your seat Please to return. ______________________

e) can What I you get? ______________________

f) is smoking There no. ______________________

g) day nice a Have. ______________________

h) coffee likes Kevin ______________________

i) student I am a. ______________________

j) a to flight want be I attendant. ______________________

Unit 9

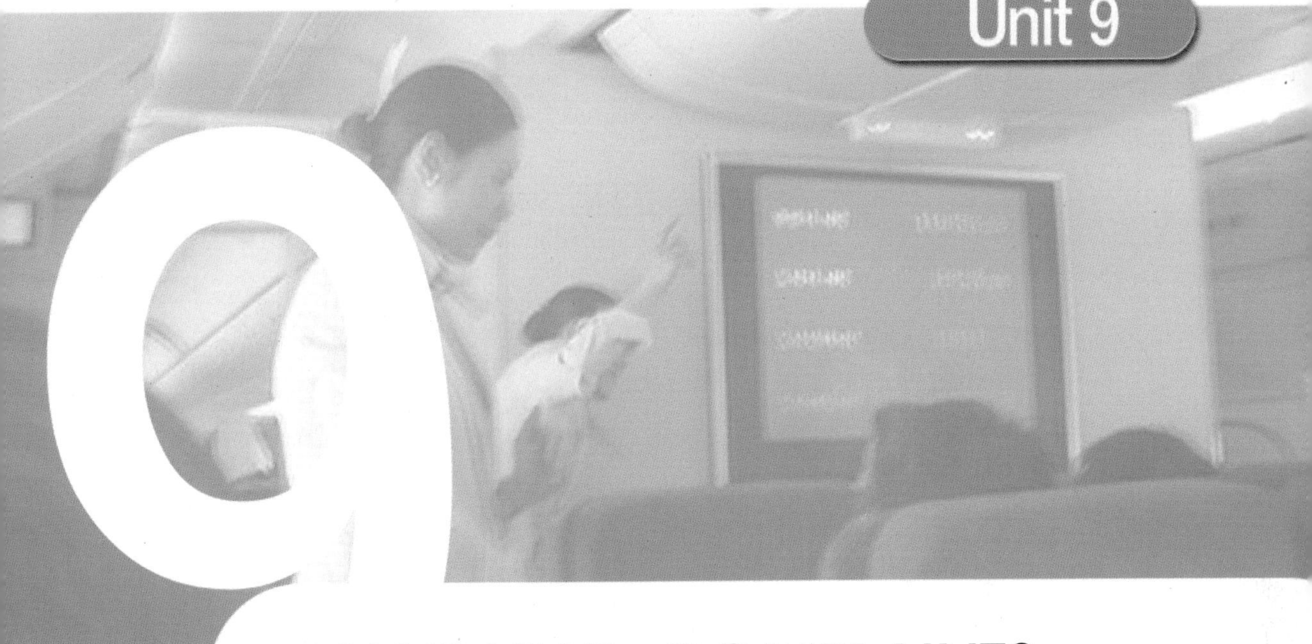

9 HANDLING COMPLAINTS AND REQUESTS

Vocabulary and Useful expressions

brewed	appreciate	urgent
aviation law	low sodium	a heart disorder
assorted fruit	bassinet	ground staff
temperature		

- This meal is not hot enough.
- I'll heat it up more for you.
- Using a cell phone is not allowed during the flight.
- I requested a low sodium meal.
- We are really sorry for the inconvenience.
- I feel chilly. Could you turn up the heat?

Dialogues

C : Cabin crew　　**P** : Passenger

Handling Complaints

Dialogue 1

P1 : Excuse me. I'm trying to get some sleep, but those little boys are making a lot of noise. Could you do something about it?

C : I'm sorry, sir. Just a moment, please. Hello, what's your name?

P2 : Johnny.

C : What's yours?

P3 : David.

C : Do you want something to drink? We have pineapple juice and tomato juice. Which one would you like?

P2 : Pineapple juice, please.

P3 : Me, too.

C : OK, I'll get you some pineapple juice. Where are your seats, boys?

Dialogue 2

P : Excuse me. This meal is not hot enough and this coffee tastes bad.

C : I'm really sorry, ma'am. I'll heat it up for you and let me bring you another cup of coffee.

(.......)

I'm sorry to have kept you waiting. Here's some freshly brewed coffee.

P : Thanks. How about the meal?

C : We are heating up your meal now. It'll be ready soon.

(.......)

Ma'am, here is your meal. I hope it is hot enough. How is it?

P : Good. Thank you.

Dialogue 3

P : Excuse me. Look at this. There is a hair in my food! You can't expect me to eat this.

C : I'm really sorry. Please let me take your tray and I'll get you another meal right away.

(.......)

Thanks for waiting. Here's another meal. Please accept our apologies.

Dialogue 4

P : Excuse me. I dropped my lipstick on the floor a few minutes ago and I can't find it. I think it rolled back.

C : Oh, let me take a look. (bends down to the floor)

P : Can you see it?

C : No, I can't. It must have rolled way back. Let me go and check at the back of the aircraft.

P : Thanks. I'd appreciate that.

(.......)

C : Is this the lipstick you were looking for?

P : Yes, it is. Where did you find it?

C : A gentleman at the back picked it up.

P : Thanks. This is my favorite one. I'd hate to lose it.

Dialogue 5

C : Excuse me, sir. Using a cell phone is not allowed during the flight.

P : Pardon?

C : Please turn off your cell phone.

P : Oh, come on! We are already off the ground. Why can't I use the phone? I really have to make an important call. It is really urgent.

C : I'm sorry, sir. Using a cell phone is not allowed during the flight. Would you please turn it off now? It is for the safe operation of our flight and in compliance with the aviation law.

P : Hmm. Alright.

C : Thank you for your cooperation, sir.

☐ Handling requests

Dialogue 6

P : Excuse me. I requested a low sodium meal when I made my reservation.

C : Could I have your name, please?

P : Angelina Adams.

C : Could you please wait for one moment? I will go and check on your meal now.

P : Sure, no problem.

(.......)

C : I'm really sorry, ma'am, our ground staff must have made a mistake. Your low sodium meal is not on board the aircraft. Please accept our apologies.

P : Oh, how could they forget it? I have a heart disorder. That's why I specifically requested the meal.

C : We are really sorry for the inconvenience. Would you like to try one of the meals we're serving, perhaps a plate of assorted fruit and vegetables?

P : Well, all right. Could you bring me a cup of milk, too?

C : Certainly, ma'am. I'll bring them right away.

(.......)

Here they are. If you need anything, please let us know.

P : Okay.

Dialogue 7

P : Excuse me. I requested a western vegetarian meal when I made my reservation.

C : Is that so, sir? Could you tell me your name, please?

P : Richard Porter.

C : Thank you. I'll go and check on your meal.

(......)

Thank you for waiting. We have the western vegetarian meal you've requested on board. It'll be ready shortly.

P : Thanks.

Dialogue 8

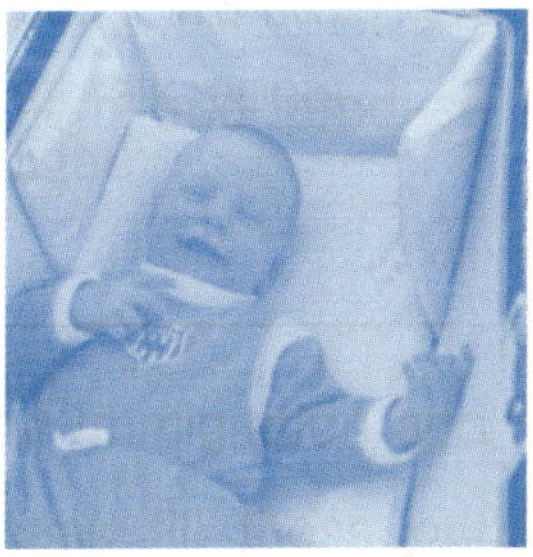

P : Miss, I have a baby here, can I use a baby bassinet, please?

Could I have a pillow and a blanket, too.

C : Of course, maam. I'll get them for you.

P : Thanks.

C : Here is a baby bassinet, a blanket and a pillow. If there's anything else I can do for you, let me know. I'll be happy to help you.

P : Thank you very much.

C : My pleasure.

(.......)

P : Hello, could you warm up this bottle, please?

C : Certainly.

(.......)

Here is the bottle. Is this warm enough?

P : Yes, thanks.

Dialogue 9

C : Did you call for me, sir?

P : Yes, I feel chilly. Could you turn up the heat?

C : I'm sorry, but we can't change the temperature in the cabin. I can get you a blanket or a hot tea, if you like.

P : Alright, then, can I have a blanket, please? Oh, and a pillow, too?

C : Yes, sir. Anything else? How about a hot tea?

P : That would be nice. Thanks.

C : If you need anything, just press the call button.

P : Okay.

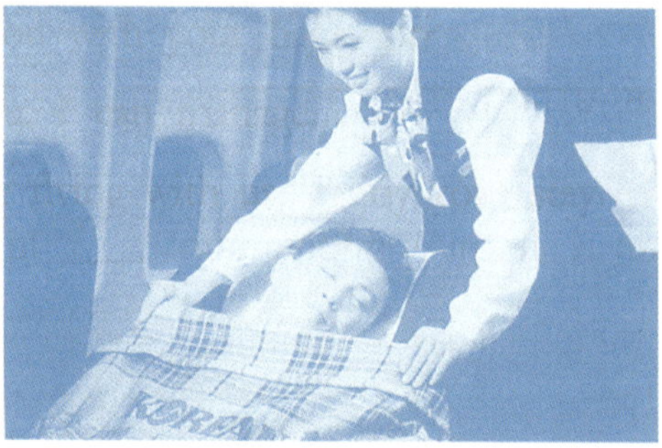

Say it in English

1. 이 식사가 충분히 뜨겁지 않아요.

2. 좀 더 뜨겁게 데워 드리겠습니다.

3. 비행 중에는 휴대전화를 사용할 수 없습니다.

4. 제가 예약할 때 저염분 식사를 신청했어요.

5. 불편을 끼쳐드려서 정말 죄송합니다.

Reading

False Alarm[3)]

For two minutes on Wednesday afternoon, passengers aboard a British Airways flight from Portugal to London prepared for a crash landing in the English Channel. "This is an emergency," said a taped message over the in-flight loudspeaker. The message then told passengers they were going to land on water. It told them to get their life jackets from their seats and wait for further instructions from the cabin crew.

The 103 passengers on flight BA32 were very frightened when the cabin crew rushed into the aisle. A flight attendant then told everyone that it was a false alarm. She had pushed the wrong button, she said.

Out of more than a dozen tapes—from announcing takeoff to selling duty-free alcohol—the flight attendant had made a mistake and chosen the message that prepares passengers for a crash landing on water, a BA spokesman explained later.

3) Roger Barnard, *Good News, Bad News* (NY:Oxford University Press, 1998), p.56

1. Use the words in the box to complete the questions.

false alarm	dozen	aisle	rush
flight attendant	crash	landling	

1) What's a(n) ________________?

It's when a plane lands in a dangerous way.

2) What does ________________ mean?

It's another way of saying hurry.

3) What's a(n) ________________?

It's someone who looks after passengers on a plane.

4) What does a(n)______________ mean?

Twelve.

5) What's a(n) ________________?

It is a long narrow passage between rows of seats.

6) What does ___________________ mean?

It's a warning that something dangerous is going to happen, but it doesn't.

2. Read the sentences below. Number them in the order the events happened. The first one has been done for you.

______ a. The message told the passengers they were going to land on water.

______ b. The passengers heard a taped message.

___1___ c. A plane took off in Portugal.

______ d. A flight attendant then explained that it was a false alarm.

______ e. The cabin crew rushed into the aisles.

______ f. It told them to get their life jackets.

______ g. The plane started to cross the English Channel.

Activities

A. Fill in the blanks with appropriate word from the box.

enough	get	be	take	requested	using	made	accept

1. I'll _______ you some pineapple juice.

2. This meal is not hot _________

3. Let me ______ a look.

4. ______ a cell phone is not allowed during the flight.

5. I __________ a low sodium meal when I made my reservation.

6. Our ground staff must have _______ a mistake.

7. Please _______ our apologies.

8. I'll ____ happy to help you.

B. Please match the words and make 8 proper phrases.

heat	bassinet
bend	staff
make	up
assorted	down
aviation	staff
heart	a call
baby	law
ground	disorders

example: 1. heat up

2. ______ ________

3. ______ ________

4. ______ ________

5. ______ ________

6. ______ ________

7. ______ ________

8. ______ ________

C. Make another expression using the following pattern.

a) I'll get you some pineapple juice.

b) I'll get you ______________________________

a) Using a cell phone is not allowed during the flight.

b) _____________ is not allowed during the flight.

a) I requested a low sodium meal when I made my reservation.

b) I requested ______________________________

a) Could you turn up the heat?

b) Could you ______________________________

a) Let me go and check at the back of the aircraft.

b) Let me go and ______________________________

a) Thank you for waiting.

b) Thank you for ________________________

If you need more activities, please refer to the appendix.

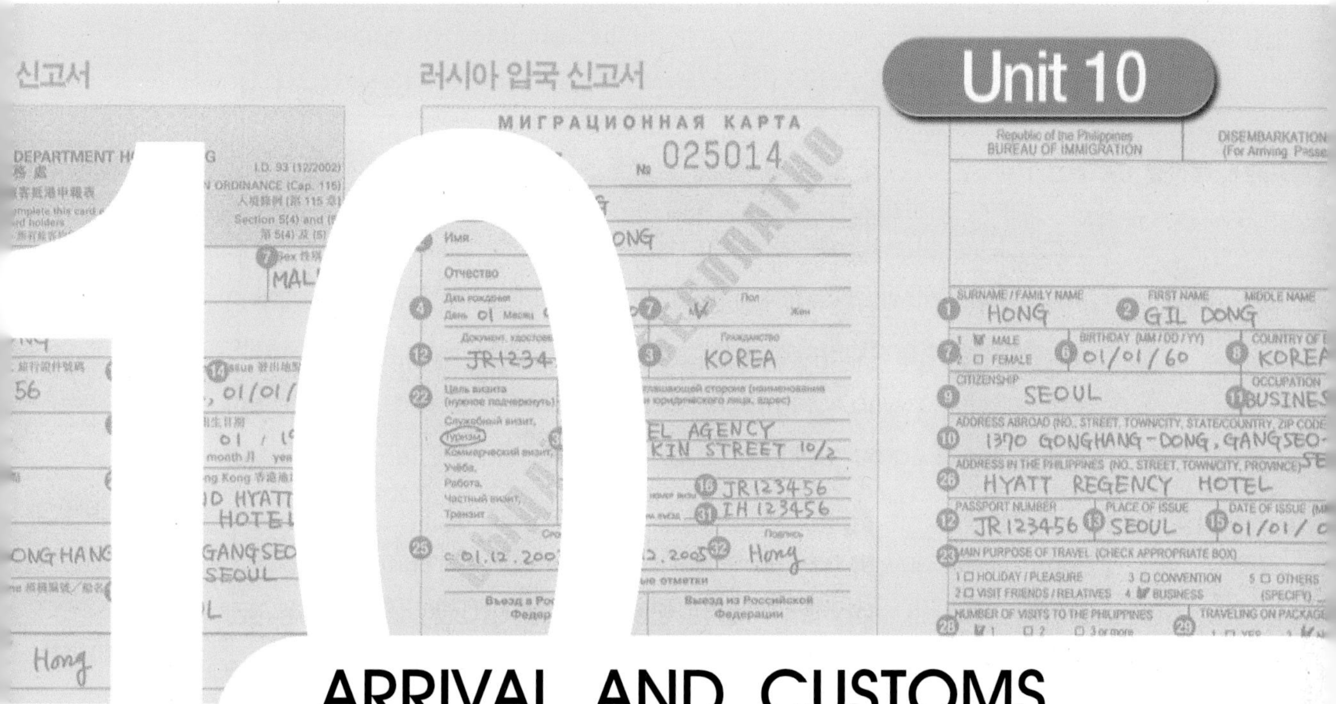

Unit 10

10 ARRIVAL AND CUSTOMS DECLARATION CARDS

Vocabulary and Useful expressions

Immigration Card	Customs Declaration Card	fill out
Embarkation Card	Disembarkation Card	items
destination	signature	complete

- Do I have to fill out this card?
- Could you help me fill it out?
- You have to write the destination and put your signature here.
- I'll be staying in Korea for one week.
- Why don't we ask the flight attendant for help?
- Thanks for your help.

Dialogues

C : Cabin crew **P** : Passenger

Dialogue 1

P : Excuse me. I just got this form and can I ask you something?

C : Sure. What can I help you with?

P : Thanks. I'll be staying in Korea for one week. Do I have to fill out this card?

C : Yes, sir. All passengers entering Korea must fill out the Embarkation Card. Do you need help filling out the form?

P : Oh. Yes, please. That would be great. Thanks.

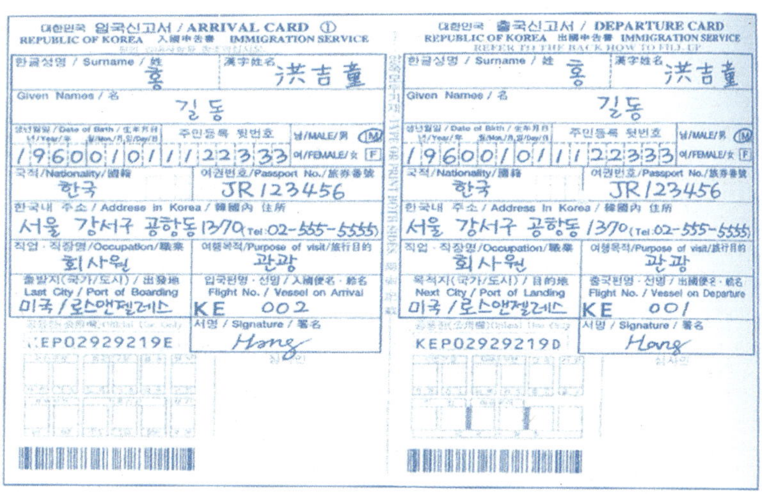

대한민국 입국신고서 / ARRIVAL CARD
REPUBLIC OF KOREA 入國申告書 IMMIGRATION SERVICE

한글성명 / Surname / 姓: 홍 | 漢字姓名: 洪吉童
Given Names / 名: 길동
생년월일 / Date of Birth: 1960 / 01 / 01 | 주민등록 뒷번호: 1122333 | 남/MALE/男 (M) | 여/FEMALE/女 F
국적/Nationality/國籍: 한국 | 여권번호/Passport No./旅券番號: JR123456
한국내 주소 / Address in Korea / 韓國內 住所: 서울 강서구 공항동 1370 (Tel: 02-555-5555)
직업 · 직장명/Occupation/職業: 회사원 | 여행목적/Purpose of visit/旅行目的: 관광
출발지(국가/도시) / 出發地 Last City / Port of Boarding: 미국/로스앤젤레스 | 입국편명 · 선명 / 入國便名 · 船名 Flight No. / Vessel on Arrival: KE 002
KEP02929219E | 서명 / Signature / 署名: Hong

대한민국 출국신고서 / DEPARTURE CARD
REPUBLIC OF KOREA 出國申告書 IMMIGRATION SERVICE

한글성명 / Surname / 姓: 홍 | 漢字姓名: 洪吉童
Given Names / 名: 길동
생년월일 / Date of Birth: 1960 / 01 / 01 | 주민등록 뒷번호: 1122333 | 남/MALE/男 (M) | 여/FEMALE/女 F
국적/Nationality/國籍: 한국 | 여권번호/Passport No./旅券番號: JR123456
한국내 주소 / Address in Korea / 韓國內 住所: 서울 강서구 공항동 1370 (Tel: 02-555-5555)
직업 · 직장명/Occupation/職業: 회사원 | 여행목적/Purpose of visit/旅行目的: 관광
목적지(국가/도시) / 目的地 Next City / Port of Landing: 미국/로스앤젤레스 | 출국편명 · 선명 / 出國便名 · 船名 Flight No. / Vessel on Departure: KE 001
KEP02929219D | 서명 / Signature / 署名: Hong

한국 출국 입국 신고서

Dialogue 2

C : Here is your disembarkation card.

P : Thanks. Could you help me fill it out?

C : Of course, sir. Here, you must write your passport number and your address.

P : Alright, and then?

C : You have to write the destination, and put your signature here. Ok, that's all you need to do.

P : That was not difficult. Thanks for you help.

Dialogue 3

C : Ma'am, this is the immigration card and the customs declaration card. Please fill these out before we land.

P : OK. After I fill out these forms, can you check them for me, please?

C : Sure, I'll be glad to.

(......)

P : I've just completed my customs declaration form. Is it all right?

C : You have to write the total value of your items, ma'am.

P : In US dollars?

C : Yes.

Dialogue 4

P1 : Hello, did you get the Immigration Card and the Customs Declaration cards?

P2 : Yes, I did.

P1 : I just got those two forms, but I need some help to fill them out. Could you help me, please?

P2 : Well, I'd love to help you but I need some help as well. Why don't we ask the flight attendant for help?

P2 : That's a good idea. I'll press the call button.

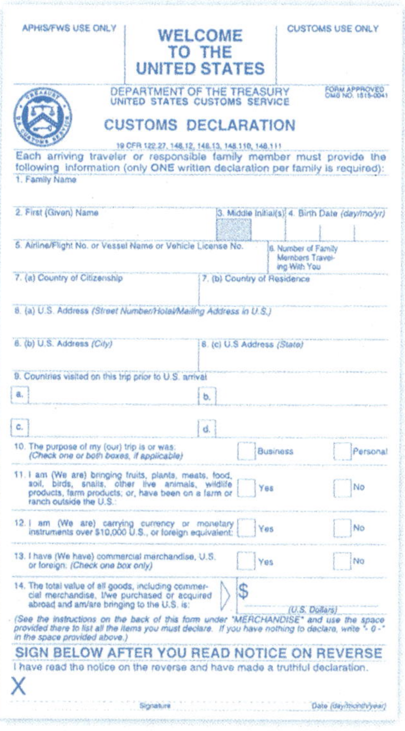

APHIS/FWS USE ONLY | WELCOME TO THE UNITED STATES | CUSTOMS USE ONLY

DEPARTMENT OF THE TREASURY
UNITED STATES CUSTOMS SERVICE

FORM APPROVED OMB NO. 1515-0041

CUSTOMS DECLARATION

19 CFR 122.27, 148.12, 148.13, 148.110, 148.111

Each arriving traveler or responsible family member must provide the following information (only ONE written declaration per family is required):

1. Family Name

2. First (Given) Name | 3. Middle Initial(s) | 4. Birth Date *(day/mo/yr)*

5. Airline/Flight No. or Vessel Name or Vehicle License No. | 6. Number of Family Members Traveling With You

7. (a) Country of Citizenship | 7. (b) Country of Residence

8. (a) U.S. Address *(Street Number/Hotel/Mailing Address in U.S.)*

8. (b) U.S. Address *(City)* | 8. (c) U.S Address *(State)*

9. Countries visited on this trip prior to U.S. arrival

a. | b.

c. | d.

10. The purpose of my (our) trip is or was: *(Check one or both boxes, if applicable)* ☐ Business ☐ Personal

11. I am (We are) bringing fruits, plants, meats, food, soil, birds, snails, other live animals, wildlife products, farm products; or, have been on a farm or ranch outside the U.S.: ☐ Yes ☐ No

12. I am (We are) carrying currency or monetary instruments over $10,000 U.S., or foreign equivalent: ☐ Yes ☐ No

13. I have (We have) commercial merchandise, U.S. or foreign: *(Check one box only)* ☐ Yes ☐ No

14. The total value of all goods, including commercial merchandise, I/we purchased or acquired abroad and am/are bringing to the U.S. is: $ *(U.S. Dollars)*

(See the instructions on the back of this form under "MERCHANDISE" and use the space provided there to list all the items you must declare. If you have nothing to declare, write "- 0 -" in the space provided above.)

SIGN BELOW AFTER YOU READ NOTICE ON REVERSE

I have read the notice on the reverse and have made a truthful declaration.

X

Signature | Date *(day/month/year)*

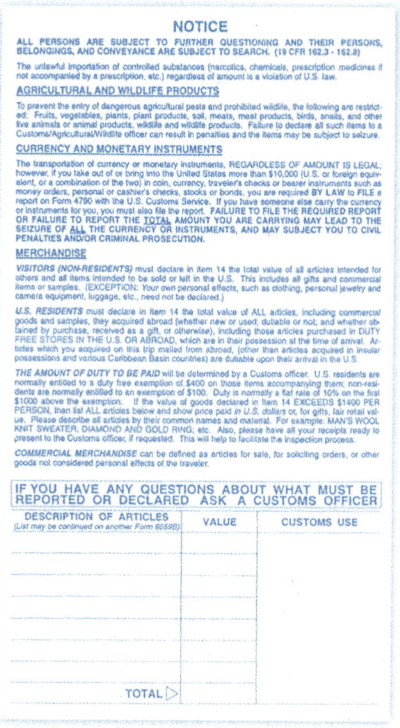

NOTICE

ALL PERSONS ARE SUBJECT TO FURTHER QUESTIONING AND THEIR PERSONS, BELONGINGS, AND CONVEYANCE ARE SUBJECT TO SEARCH. (19 CFR 162.3 - 162.8)

The unlawful importation of controlled substances (narcotics, chemicals, prescription medicines if not accompanied by a prescription, etc.) regardless of amount is a violation of U.S. law.

AGRICULTURAL AND WILDLIFE PRODUCTS

To prevent the entry of dangerous agricultural pests and prohibited wildlife, the following are restricted: Fruits, vegetables, plants, plant products, soil, meats, meat products, birds, snails, and other live animals or animal products, wildlife and wildlife products. Failure to declare all such items to a Customs/Agricultural/Wildlife officer can result in penalties and the items may be subject to seizure.

CURRENCY AND MONETARY INSTRUMENTS

The transportation of currency or monetary instruments, REGARDLESS OF AMOUNT IS LEGAL; however, if you take out of or bring into the United States more than $10,000 (U.S. or foreign equivalent, or a combination of the two) in coin, currency, traveler's checks or bearer instruments such as money orders, personal or cashier's checks, stocks or bonds, you are required BY LAW to FILE a report on Form 4790 with the U.S. Customs Service. If you have someone else carry the currency or instruments for you, you must also file the report. FAILURE TO FILE THE REQUIRED REPORT OR FAILURE TO REPORT THE TOTAL AMOUNT YOU ARE CARRYING MAY LEAD TO THE SEIZURE OF ALL THE CURRENCY OR INSTRUMENTS, AND MAY SUBJECT YOU TO CIVIL PENALTIES AND/OR CRIMINAL PROSECUTION.

MERCHANDISE

VISITORS (NON-RESIDENTS) must declare in item 14 the total value of all articles intended for others and all items intended to be sold or left in the U.S. This includes all gifts and commercial items or samples. (EXCEPTION: *Your own* personal effects, such as clothing, personal jewelry and camera equipment, luggage, etc., need not be declared.)

U.S. RESIDENTS must declare in item 14 the total value of ALL articles, including commercial goods and samples, they acquired abroad (whether new or used; dutiable or not; and whether obtained by purchase, received as a gift, or otherwise), including those articles purchased in DUTY FREE STORES IN THE U.S. OR ABROAD, which are in their possession at the time of arrival. Articles which you acquired on this trip mailed from abroad, (other than articles acquired in insular possessions and various Caribbean Basin countries) are dutiable upon their arrival in the U.S.

THE AMOUNT OF DUTY TO BE PAID will be determined by a Customs officer. U.S. residents are normally entitled to a duty free exemption of $400 on those items accompanying them; non-residents are normally entitled to an exemption of $100. Duty is normally a flat rate of 10% on the first $1000 above the exemption. If the value of goods declared in item 14 EXCEEDS $1400 PER PERSON, then list ALL articles below and show price paid *in U.S. dollars* or, for gifts, fair retail value. Please describe all articles by their common names and material. For example: MAN'S WOOL KNIT SWEATER; DIAMOND AND GOLD RING; etc. Also, please have all your receipts ready to present to the Customs officer, if requested. This will help to facilitate the inspection process.

COMMERCIAL MERCHANDISE can be defined as articles for sale, for soliciting orders, or other goods not considered personal effects of the traveler.

IF YOU HAVE ANY QUESTIONS ABOUT WHAT MUST BE REPORTED OR DECLARED ASK A CUSTOMS OFFICER

DESCRIPTION OF ARTICLES *(List may be continued on another Form 6059B)*	VALUE	CUSTOMS USE
TOTAL ▷		

세관신고서 미국

Say it in English

1. 이 카드를 작성해야만 합니까?

2. 한국에 일주일동안 머물려고 합니다.

3. 승무원에게 도움을 요청하는 것이 어때요?

4. 도와주셔서 감사합니다.

5. 여기에 사인하십시오.

Reading

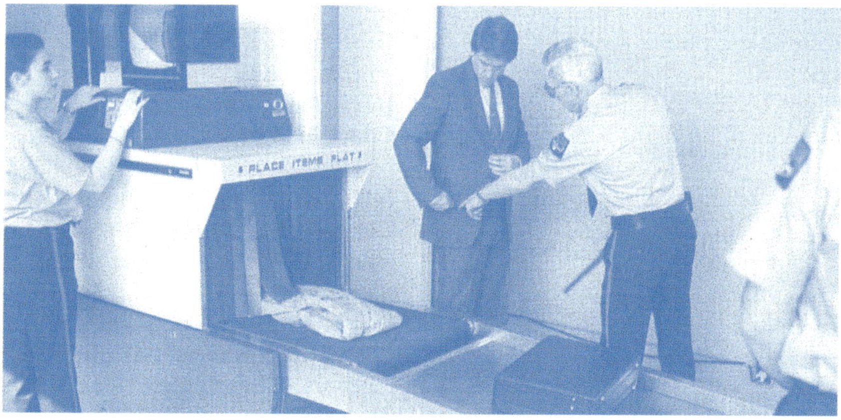

1. Before we are allowed to enter a foreign country, whether we travel by land, sea, or air, we must go through the customs. This means that our baggage must be examined by a customs official to see that we are not bringing in any articles upon which duty should be paid, and that, if we have such articles, we pay the necessary duty. We are usually asked to make a declaration about what we have in our baggage. If we have any dutiable goods we are expected to declare them and produce them.

2. Announcement: "We will be passing out Immigration and Customs Declaration Cards to all of you. Please fill these out before we land. You must give them to the Immigration and Customs Officials at the airport. We'll be happy to help you fill them out. Thank you."

Mark T if it is true and F if it is false.

1. When we enter a foreign country by airplane, we must go through customs. (T / F)

2. The airline's ground staff examines our baggage to see if we have brought any dutiable goods. (T / F)

3. If we have any articles upon which duty should be paid, we should declare them and produce them to the customs officials. (T / F)

4. We don't need to fill out the Immigration and Customs Declaration Cards before we land. (T / F)

Activities

A. Look for the words in the Word List.

F	O	R	M	S	J	P	A	S	S	P	O	R	T	J	W	E	C	R	B
Y	W	P	I	M	M	I	G	R	A	T	I	O	N	C	A	R	D	T	U
E	D	E	S	T	I	N	A	T	I	O	N	N	E	N	K	Z	B	G	B
S	I	G	N	A	T	U	R	E	B	T	O	T	A	L	V	A	L	U	E
Z	Y	E	M	B	A	R	K	A	T	I	O	N	C	A	R	D	T	L	F
N	V	H	S	J	V	Q	P	A	S	S	E	N	G	E	R	S	Q	T	O
J	J	Q	N	B	I	T	E	M	S	Z	P	X	S	E	Z	G	K	X	K

Word List :

destination	embarkation card	forms
immigration card	items	passengers
passport	signature	total value

B. Fill in the blanks with the proper words in the box.

completed	fill	glad	need	staying

1. I'll be _______ to.
2. Can you help me _____ it out?
3. I'll be _____ in Korea for one week.
4. Do I _____ to fill out this card?
5. I've just ________ my Customs Declaration Form.

If you need more activities, please refer to the appendix.

11 PREPARATION FOR LANDING

Vocabulary and Useful expressions

shortly local time time difference

estimated time of arrival lavatory complete stop

connecting flight

- We'll be landing shortly.
- What's the local time in Seoul now?
- Australia is one hour ahead of Seoul.
- What's the estimated time of arrival in Seoul?
- Do you mind keeping your bag under your seat?
- Everyone must remain seated until the plane comes to a complete stop.
- It's for passenger safety.

Dialogues

C : Cabin crew P : Passenger

Dialogue 1

C : Excuse me. We'll be landing shortly. May I have your earphones, please?

P : Here they are. What's the local time in Seoul?

C : Well, it's four o'clock in the morning. Would you return your seat to the upright position and keep your seat belt fastened for landing, please?

P : Yes, of course. Do you know the time difference between Seoul and Australia?

C : Australia is one hour ahead of Seoul.

P : Thanks.

Dialogue 2

C : Excuse me. May I have your blanket, please? We'll be landing soon.

P : Sure, here it is.

C : Sir, would you mind returning your seat back to the upright position and closing your tray table?

P : Alright. I'll do that. Excuse me, what's the estimated time of arrival in Seoul?

C : It's ten o'clock in the afternoon, local time.

P : I see. Thanks.

Dialogue 3

C : Ma'am, have you finished your drink?

P : Yes, I have.

C : Do you mind keeping your bag under your seat? It might fall during landing.

P : No, not at all, I'll keep it under my seat. Can I have one more cup of orange juice, please?

C : I'm sorry. We've closed the bar for landing. Would you please close your tray table?

P : Sure.

C : Thank you.

Dialogue 4

C : Excuse me, sir. Would you please return to your seat? We'll be landing shortly.

P : Can I use the lavatory now?

C : Yes, go ahead.

P : Thanks.

C : Please remember to fasten your seatbelt when you return to your seat.

P : Ok, I will.

Dialogue 5

C : I'm sorry sir, would you please sit down? The captain requests that everyone remain seated until the plane comes to a complete stop.

P : Look, I'm in a hurry.

C : Yes, but it is for passenger safety.

P : I am worried about my connecting flight.

C : When is your next flight?

P : It is departing in 20 minutes.

C : Do you know which gate?

P : Yes, it is on my boarding pass.

Say it in English

1. 곧 착륙합니다.

2. 서울 현지시각은 몇 시 입니까?

3. 서울 도착예정시간은 몇시죠?

4. 비행기가 완전히 멈출때까지,

5. 승객의 안전을 위한 것입니다.

Reading

Announcements :

1. "Ladies and gentlemen, may I have your attention, please? We will be landing at Incheon Airport in twenty minutes. Please fasten your seat belt and return your seat and tray table to the upright position. All portable electronic devices must be turned off until the plane comes to a complete stop. Thank you."

2. "Ladies and gentlemen, please remain in your seats until the aircraft comes to a complete stop. The local time is 11:30 a.m. All passengers leaving the aircraft at this time are requested to have their passports, Customs Declaration Forms and Disembarkation Cards ready for inspection by the authorities. Please make sure you have all your belongings with you. We hope you have enjoyed your flight. Thanks for flying with us today."

Answer the following questions.

1. When will the plane be landing at Incheon Airport?

2. What are the three things the passengers have to do before landing?

3. What must be turned off until the plane stops completely?

4. What are the electronic devices passengers are likely to bring on the plane?

5. What do the passengers have to take with them when leaving the aircraft?

Activities

A. Fill in the blanks with appropriate words from the box.

please remember	difference	keeping	have
fall	return		

1. Would you ___________your seat to the upright position ?
2. What's the time ___________ between Seoul and Australia?
3. ________ you finished your drink?
4. Do you mind _________your bag under your seat?
5. It might ___________ during landing.
6. _________ to fasten your seat belt when you return to your seat.

B. Unscramble the tiles to reveal a phrase.

1.

diff	time	er	ence

2.

ti	cal	me	lo

3.

of	val	time	mated	arri	esti

C. Match the answers to the following questions.

1) May I have your blanket, please? We'll be landing soon.
2) What's the estimated time of arrival in Seoul?
3) Do you know the time difference between Seoul and Australia?
4) Have you finished your drink?
5) Do you mind keeping your bag under your seat?
6) When is your next flight?

_______ a) No, not at all,
_______ b) Yes, I have.
_______ c) It's ten o'clock in the afternoon, local time.
_______ d) It is departing in 20 minutes.
_______ e) Australia is one hour ahead of Seoul.
_______ f) Sure, here it is.

Unit 12

ARRIVAL

Vocabulary and Useful expressions

at last	fantastic	pleasant
safety	onward	belongings
transit	deplane	

- At last, we're in Seattle.
- I hope you enjoyed your flight.
- Did you enjoy the flight?
- Enjoy your stay in Jeju Island.
- Thank you for flying with us.
- I hope to see you again.

Dialogues

C : Cabin crew　　P : Passenger

Dialogue 1

C : At last, we're in Seattle. I hope you enjoyed your flight, sir.

P : Thanks to you, it was fantastic. Thank you.

C : You're welcome. We hope to see you again. Good bye. Have a pleasant stay in Seattle.

P : Thank you. Good bye.

Dialogue 2

P : Excuse me, could you get my coat, please? I gave it to you when I boarded the plane.

C : Yes, sir. Just a moment, please.

(......)

Here is your coat. Did you enjoy the flight?

P : Yes, it was great. Thanks.

C : You're welcome. I hope to see you again.

Dialogue 3

C : May I help you with your bags, ma'am?

P : Oh, thank you.

C : You're welcome.

P : Sorry, but I have one more bag in the overhead compartment. Could you get it out for me?

C : No problem. Is this bag yours?

P : No, the red one is mine.

C : It must be this one, then. (heading to the exit) This way, ma'am.

P : Thanks a lot.

Dialogue 4

C : May I help you with your bags, sir?

P : No, thank you. I can manage.

C : Thank you for flying with us. Enjoy your stay in Jeju Island.

P : Thanks. Bye.

Dialogue 5

P : (stands up to get the bag out of the overhead compartment.)

C : Sir, please remain seated until the plane comes to a complete stop and the seatbelt sign has been turned off.

P : Oh, alright. I thought we had arrived at the terminal. Why aren't we moving?

C : We are waiting for another plane to depart.

P : I see.

Say it in English

1. 마침내 시애틀에 도착했습니다.

2. 비행기 여행이 즐거웠습니까?

3. 제주도에서 즐거운 시간을 보내기 바랍니다.

4. 저희 비행기를 이용해 주셔서 감사합니다.

5. 다시 뵙길 바랍니다.

Reading

Announcements:

1. "Ladies and gentlemen, we have just landed at Incheon Airport. The local time is seven o'clock in the morning. For your safety, please remain seated until the captain has turned off the seat belt sign. Be careful when opening the overhead compartment, since bags may have shifted during the flight. Please check to make sure that you have not left any items behind. On behalf of the entire flight crew, we would like to express our sincere thanks to all of you for flying United Airlines. It has been our pleasure serving you and we hope to see you again soon. If you have onward or return booking with United Airlines, please reconfirm your flight 72 hours before your departure. Thank you for flying with us today, and we wish you a pleasant stay in Seoul."

2. "Thank you for waiting, ladies and gentlemen. You may now exit through the forward door and please make sure to take all your belongings with you when you deplane. We wish you a pleasant day and thank you once again for flying Air Canada."

3. "Ladies and gentlemen, passengers continuing on to New York are requested to obtain a transit card after deplaning and proceed to the transit area. You may keep your hand baggage in the overhead compartments, but please be sure to take your boarding pass, passport and other valuables with you. We will be on the ground for about an hour. Boarding will be announced in the transit area. Thank you."

Answer the following questions.

1. Where did the plane land?

2. Which airline are they traveling with?

3. What's the local time in Seoul?

4. Why do the passengers have to be careful when opening the overhead compartment?

5. What kind of card are the transit passengers requested to obtain?

6. How long will the plane be on the ground?

Activities

A. Fill in the blanks with the proper words from the box.

for to with in

1. We hope _____ see you again.
2. Have a pleasant stay ____ Seattle.
3. May I help you _______ your bags, ma'am?
4. Could you get it out _____me?
5. Thank you for flying _____ us.
6. Enjoy your stay ______ Jeju.

B. Put the sentences in the correct order.

1. you thanks to it fantastic was.

   ____

2. you could my get coat please?

   ____

3. help may I you your bags with ma'am?

   ____

4. flying you for with thank us.

   ____

5. in your enjoy stay Jeju.

   ____

C. Choose the matching sentences from the box.

1. open the overhead compartment,	2. any items behind.
3. pleasure serving you	4. seated
5. to see you again soon.	6. shifted during the flight.
7. we would like to express our sincere thanks to you.	
8. turned off the seat belt sign.	

a) For your safety, please remain ____________________

b) until the captain has ____________________

c) Be careful when you ____________________

d) since bags may have ____________________

e) Please check that you have not left ____________________

f) On behalf of the entire flight crew, ____________________

g) It has been our ____________________

h) We hope ____________________

Unit 13

13 REFINING YOUR FLIGHT ATTENDANT CONVERSATION SKILLS

Vocabulary and Useful expressions

souvenir	misunderstood	apologize
business	explain	window shade
pleasure	close	familiar

- What do you need?
- Can you please explain that?
- I am not familiar with that.
- I will get one of our English speaking flight attendants to help you.
- It's been a long flight.
- Are you traveling on business or for pleasure today?
- I will see what I can find as a souvenir.

Dialogues

C : Cabin crew　　P : Passenger

Dialogue 1

P : Excuse me, I need a Kleenex.

C : I'm sorry, ma'am. I don't understand. What do you need?

P : A Kleenex.

C : I'm very sorry, can you please explain that? I am not familiar with Kleenex.

P : Oh, I mean a tissue. I spilled a little bit of water.

C : I understand now. I'll be right back.

P : Thank you.

Dialogue 2

P : Can you help me? I ordered a vegetarian meal and I got this beef dish.

C : Yes, this is a beef dish, sir.

P : No, no. I want a vegetarian meal. I don't want beef.

C : I apologize. I misunderstood. I will get one of our English speaking flight attendants to help you right away.

P : Thank you.

Dialogue 3

C : How are you doing today?

P : I'm fine, but a little tired. It's been a long flight.

C : Yes, I know, but we have only another hour. Are you traveling on business or for pleasure today?

P : I am going to visit my grandchildren. I haven't seen them in months.

C : That's very nice. How old are they?

P : Here is a photo of them. My granddaughter is three and my grandson is seven. He loves airplanes. Can I take this magazine to show him?

C : They are so cute! I will see what I can find as a souvenir for your grandson.

P : That would be great! Thank you so much. He will be very excited.

Dialogue 4

P : Can you tell me where we are?

C : Yes. If you open your window shade, you will be able to see the Rocky Mountains. We are flying over the Canadian side right now.

P : Wow, that's beautiful. I have never seen the Rockies before! How long before we land in Vancouver? We must be close.

C : We should be landing in about 30 minutes. Is this your first trip to Canada?

P : Yes, I am so excited to see it.

C : Well, enjoy your stay!

P : Thank you very much. I will!

Say it in English

1. 그것을 설명해 주시겠어요?

2. 무엇이 필요하십니까?

3. 긴 비행기여행 이었습니다.

4. 영어를 잘하는 승무원을 데려와서 당신을 도와 드리도록 하겠습니다.

5. 기념품이 될 만한 것을 찾아보겠습니다.

Reading

Flight attendants should always remember that they act as representatives of their country and their airline. You will often be the first contact that a traveler has with people from your country, so you should always be friendly to the passengers. They will appreciate a warm smile and a caring attitude. Try to answer questions with more than one word and address your passengers as 'sir' or 'ma'am'. To ask for and receive, 'please', 'thank you' and 'you're welcome' are important phrases. If there is a problem, always be polite and apologize sincerely for any error or misunderstanding. Passengers always remember good service and the quality of their experience onboard depends on you.

Answer the following questions.

1. What should you say when asking a passenger for an item?
   a) Give that to me!
   b) Could I please have that?
   c) What do you want?

2. When a passenger says 'thank you', what should your response be?
   a) No response.
   b) Uh.
   c) You're welcome.

3. When addressing a male passenger you should say:
    a) Excuse me, sir.
    b) Hey you!
    c) Hello?

4. What can you say if there has been a misunderstanding that has made a passenger angry?
    a) Be quiet. I am angry too!
    b) I'm very sorry for the misunderstanding. I will do my best to fix the problem.
    c) I'm very busy.

5. What can you say if a passenger says something you don't understand?
    a) Nothing, just walk away quickly.
    b) I don't know.
    c) I'm very sorry but I don't understand you. I will get one of the English speaking flight attendants to help you right away.

Activities

A. Answer the following questions.

1. What are some things that you might talk with a passenger about to make their flight more comfortable and enjoyable?

   ____________ ______________ _________________

2. What can you do if you do not understand a passenger?

   ____________ ______________ _________________

3. How can you make sure that a passenger sees that you are friendly?

   ____________ ______________ _________________

4. What are some polite words that you can use in conversation?

   ____________ ______________ _________________

5. What are some things that you should not talk about to a passenger?

   ____________ ______________ _________________

B. Put the vocabulary words into Korean and use them in an English sentence.

	Korean	Use it in a sentence.
souvenir	______________	__________________________
misunderstood	______________	__________________________
apologize	______________	__________________________
business	______________	__________________________
explain	______________	__________________________
window shade	______________	__________________________
pleasure	______________	__________________________
souvenir	______________	__________________________
close	______________	__________________________

C. Use the vocabulary words to complete the puzzle.

Across

3. Well known.
6. Something brought back as a reminder of a place.
8. Another word for work.
9. Not correctly understood.

Down

1. Another word for fun.
2. Near
4. To say that you are sorry for something.
5. A covering for the window to keep the light out.
7. To make the meaning clear.

APPENDIX

More Activities

Unit 1

Aircraft Type and Seat Position

Aircraft Type
B 747-400 / 300 (version 7441/ 7431)

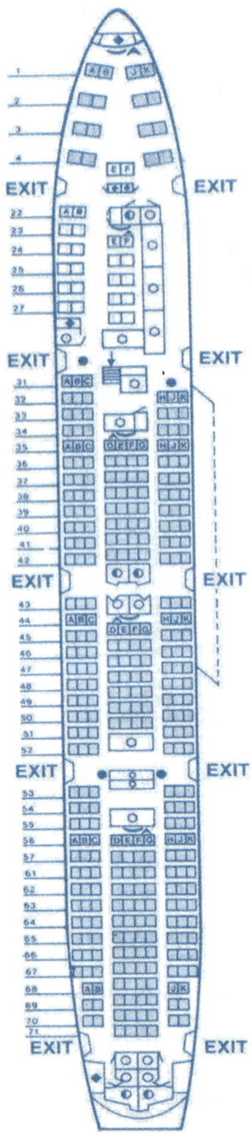

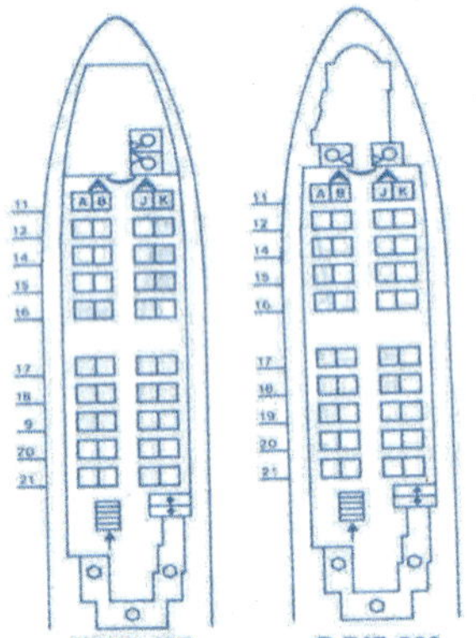

Upper deck

Aircraft Type Code 744/743

Seat plan

Royal First Class Row 1-4	18 seats
Royal Executive Class Upper deck Row 11-21	40 seats
Royal Executive Class Main deck Row 22-27	22 seats
Economy Row 31-71	325 seats

Facility and Comfort

- ◆ Coat room
- ○ Toilette
- ◐ Toilette with diaper change board
- ⬡ Galley
- ^ Baby bassinets
- ‿ Video screen
- ● Video monitor

Carry - on bagage and Safety

Carry-on baggage to be placed in overhead locker or under the seat in front only

Choose the correct meaning of each word.

aisle	boarding pass	seat
stewardess	passenger	steward

_____________ : an official card issued by an airline which allows a person to board an airplane, etc.

_____________ : a female steward on a ship, airplane, etc.

_____________ : someone whose job is to look after the needs of passengers on a ship or aircraft.

_____________ : a traveller in a vehicle, boat, airplane, etc driven, sailed or piloted by someone else.

_____________ : a passage between rows of seats, for example in an aircraft, theatre, or church.

_____________ : anything designed or intended for sitting on.

Unit 5.

SIMPLE PAST

- Past tense is used to express events that have already happened. To change a sentence from present to past, you must change the verb to its past tense form. Most verbs can be changed to past tense by adding –ed but there are some verbs that are irregular. Irregular verbs are each conjugated differently.

Regular verbs:

laugh > laughed	wash > washed	watch > watched
play > played	work > worked	help > helped

Irregular verbs:

drink > drank	eat > ate	wake > woke
sleep > slept	run > ran	keep > kept

Change the following sentences to past tense. Replace the verb in (brackets) with the correct past tense verb from the list below. Circle the verbs that are regular.

bought	paid	woke	ate	was
went	had	turned	returned	took
announced	slept	forgot	landed	drank

1) The plane (take) off two hours late.
2) Jenny (buy) make-up at the duty-free shop.
3) Janice (sleep) on the plane.
4) Sarah (go) through security.
5) James (drink) three cups of tea.
6) They (pay) $30 because one bag (be) very heavy.
7) The captain (announce) that the passengers(have) to put on their seat belts.
8) Rachel (wake) up when they (turn) on the lights.
9) Shelly almost (forget) her bag when the plane (land).
10) Anna (eat) all her meal before the flight attendant (return).

Unit 6.

Find the words from the box.

V	B	S	U	D	C	C	E	D	P	T	R	R	Z	F
N	E	J	E	A	P	N	V	C	X	L	Y	R	C	M
G	H	G	R	N	I	F	A	Q	J	E	F	T	N	Q
A	A	T	E	Z	O	T	A	X	G	B	E	T	L	U
J	V	L	A	T	A	H	S	E	A	T	B	A	C	K
G	V	G	L	L	A	M	P	E	H	A	L	B	H	Q
X	A	E	O	E	I	R	T	R	H	E	I	E	A	D
M	D	G	G	W	R	O	I	E	A	S	L	V	N	T
Q	U	Q	S	A	M	G	A	A	M	E	Y	E	N	L
E	H	E	D	E	N	D	Y	I	N	K	F	R	E	O
R	E	F	R	E	S	H	M	E	N	T	S	A	L	H
F	T	N	T	E	K	N	A	L	B	G	M	G	I	O
Y	O	N	T	Q	P	I	L	L	O	W	E	E	A	C
N	C	P	D	I	J	A	Y	K	J	D	A	S	V	L
A	E	E	L	B	A	T	Y	A	R	T	L	F	M	A

ALCOHOL	ALLERGY	BLANKET
CART	CHANNEL	EARPHONES
MAGAZINE	MEAL	CATALOGUE
HEADSET	REFRESHMENTS	PILLOW
SEATBACK	VEGAN	REMOTE
SEATBELT	TRAY TABLE	VEGETARIAN
BEVERAGE		

Unit 9.

There are various kinds of meals served in the airplane according to age, religion and preference.

Various Meals[4]

1. Vegetarian Meals

	Meat	Dairy	Egg	Root Vegetable
Western Vegetarian Meal		√	√	√
Strict Vegetarian Meal				√
Asian Vegetarian Meal		√		√
Strict Asian Vegetarian Meal				
Oriental Vegetarian Meal				√

Oriental Vegetarian Meal is available on Seoul departure flights only.

4) Source : www.Koreanair.com 12월 22일 기준

2. Health Conscious Meals

Bland Meal	For passengers with digestive difficulties or in the recovery stage after operation	Soft meals prepared by boiling or parboiling without strong spices
Diabetic Meal	For diabetics	Meals with no sugar or honey
Low Fat Meal	For passengers with heart disorders or over-weight	Meals prepared by removing fat or fatty substance from meat
Low Protein Meal	For passengers with kidney or liver disorders	Meals which are not salty with no meat stock or nuts
Low Sodium	For passengers with heart disorders or hypertension	Meals with no salt or salty substance
Low Calorie Meal	On diet	Meals based on the consumption of 1200kcal per day
High Fiber Meal	Chronic constipation	Meals with grain, fruit or vegetables with plenty of fiber
None Lactose	passengers with lactose intolerance	Meals with no milk or lactose
Low Purine Meal	Purine metabolism disorders such as arthritis	Meals with limited Purine and fat

Peanut Allergy Passenger Information

As food ingredients containing peanut element, peanut oil or other peanut products are commonly used worldwide, we can not guarantee peanut-free snacks and meals even if we do not use peanuts in our catering production process.

3. Religious Meals

Moslem Meal	Hindu Meal	Kosher Meal
- Meal prepared according to Halal rules - No pork or alcohol	- Meal prepared for Indian people. - No beef or pork	- Prepared according to Jewish dietary rules and made after a traditional ceremony - Purchased from reputable manufacturers

4. Baby/Infant Meal

Passengers	Food provided
Infants between the ages of 9 months to 2 years	Powdered milk, strained food and orange juice (Since common brands are provided during flight, if you have a selected brand of juice or milk, please prepare individually.)

5. Child Meal

Flights Leaving Seoul	Flights Arriving at Seoul
Zajangmyun (noodle with brown sauce), Omelet rice, Kimbab (Korean sushi), Sandwiches, Hamburger, Pizza, Spaghetti, Chicken nuggets	Hamburger, Pizza, Spaghetti, Chicken nuggets

Passengers: Children from age 2 to 12

Unit 10.

Practice with your partner.

Thanks for + noun

Thanks for your help.

Thanks for your concern.

Thanks for your hospitality.

Can (Could) you help me ~ ?

Could you help me fill it out?

Could you help me find my cell phone?

Can you help me find him?

Can you help me with these boxes?

You have to + infinitive (You must ~)

You have to write the total value of your items.

You must write the total value of your items.

You have to write your passport number and your address.

You must write your passport number and your address.

I have to leave now.

I must leave now.

HOW TO FILL OUT IMMIGRATION DOCUMENTS

출입국 신고서 작성

일본 입국 신고서

外国人入国記録 DISEMBARKATION CARD FOR FOREIGNER ①

E.D. No. 出入国記録番号 HI 5193016 区分 21

① 氏名（漢字）	氏 洪	② 名 吉童	
(Name)	Family Name HONG	Given Names GIL DONG	
③ 国籍 Nationality as shown on passport	KOREA	④ 生年月日 Date of Birth	Day日 01 Month月 01 Year年 60 ⑦ 男 Male ✓ 女 Female
⑩ 現住所 Home Address	国名 Country name 都市名 City name 1370 GONGHANG-DONG, GANGSEO-GU, SEOUL KOREA	⑪ 職業 Occupation	BUSINESSMAN
⑫ 旅券番号 Passport number	JR123456	⑱ 航空機便名・船名 Last flight No./Vessel KE 701	⑲ 乗機地 Which airport did you board this flight or ship? INCHEON
⑳ 渡航目的 Purpose of visit	☐ 観光 Tourism ☑ 商用 Business ☐ 親族訪問 Visiting relatives ☐ トランジット Transit ☐ その他 Others ( )		㉔ 日本滞在予定期間 Intended Length of stay in Japan: Years 年 Month 月 5 Days 日
㉖ 日本の連絡先 Intended address in Japan	SHINJUKU HOTEL, TOKYO	TEL ㉗ 1234-5678	

官用欄 Official Use Only　裏面を見てください。See the back→　CL/証

KA1HI519301621

カード①とカード②の太線内を入国時に記入して下さい。Please fill in CARD ① and CARD ② (inside bold line) when entering Japan.

중국 입국 신고서

ENTRY CARD FOR FOREIGN TRAVELLERS

PLEASE COMPLETE IN ENGLISH. FILL IN ☐ WITH ✓

① Family Name	HONG	⑤ Date of Birth	YEAR MONTH DAY 19600101	OFFICIAL USE ONLY
② Given Names	GILDONG	⑦ Male ✓ Female ☐		证件种类 签证种类
⑫ Passport No.	JR123456	③ Nationality	KOREA	
⑯ Visa No.	123456	㉑ Your Main Reason for Coming to China (one only)		
⑰ Place of Visa Issuance	SEOUL	Convention / Conference ☐	Business ✓	
⑱ Flight No. Ship Name Train No.	KE 851	Employment ☐	Settle down ☐	
		Visiting friends or relatives ☐		
⑲ From	SEOUL, KOREA	Outing /in leisure ☐	Study ☐	
		Return home ☐	Others ☐	
㉖ Intended Address in China	ABC HOTEL, BEIJING			公安部出入境管理局监制

I declare the information I have given is true, correct and complete. I understand incorrect or untrue answer to any questions may have serious consequences. ㉜ SIGNATURE Hong ㉝ Date of Entry YEAR MONTH DAY 20050601

입국카드(Embarkation card for foreigners)

홍콩 입국 신고서

IMMIGRATION DEPARTMENT HONG KONG
香港入境事務處
ARRIVAL CARD 旅客抵港申報表
I.D. 93 (12/2002)
IMMIGRATION ORDINANCE (Cap. 115)
入境條例 (第 115 章)
Section 5(4) and (5)
第 5(4) 及 (5) 條
All travellers should complete this card except Hong Kong Identity Card holders
除香港身份證持有人外，所有旅客均須填寫此申報表

1 Family name (in capitals) 姓 (請用正楷填寫): HONG
7 Sex 性別: MALE
2 Given names (in capitals) 名 (請用正楷填寫): GIL DONG
12 Travel document No. 旅行證件號碼: JR123456
13 Place and date 14 of issue 簽出地點及日期: SEOUL, 01/01/06
3 Nationality 國籍: KOREA
4 Date of birth 出生日期: 01 / 01 / 1960 (day 日 month 月 year 年)
8 Place of birth 出生地點: SEOUL
26 Address in Hong Kong 香港地址: GRAND HYATT HOTEL
10 Home address 住址: 1370 GONGHANG-DONG, GANGSEO-GU SEOUL
18 Flight No./Ship's name 班機編號／船名: KE 603
19 From 來自: SEOUL
32 Signature of traveller 旅客簽署: Hong

Please write clearly 請用端正字體填寫
Do not fold 切勿摺疊

ND611196

필리핀 입국 신고서

Republic of the Philippines
BUREAU OF IMMIGRATION
DISEMBARKATION CARD (For Arriving Passengers)

1 SURNAME / FAMILY NAME: HONG
2 FIRST NAME: GIL DONG
MIDDLE NAME:
7 1 ☑ MALE 2 ☐ FEMALE
6 BIRTHDAY (MM / DD / YY): 01/01/60
8 COUNTRY OF BIRTH: KOREA
9 CITIZENSHIP: SEOUL
11 OCCUPATION: BUSINESSMAN
10 ADDRESS ABROAD (NO., STREET, TOWN/CITY, STATE/COUNTRY, ZIP CODE): 1370 GONGHANG-DONG, GANGSEO-GU, SEOUL
26 ADDRESS IN THE PHILIPPINES (NO., STREET, TOWN/CITY, PROVINCE): HYATT REGENCY HOTEL
12 PASSPORT NUMBER: JR123456
13 PLACE OF ISSUE: SEOUL
15 DATE OF ISSUE (MM / DD / YY): 01/01/06
23 MAIN PURPOSE OF TRAVEL (CHECK APPROPRIATE BOX)
1 ☐ HOLIDAY / PLEASURE 2 ☐ VISIT FRIENDS / RELATIVES 3 ☐ CONVENTION 4 ☑ BUSINESS 5 ☐ OTHERS (SPECIFY)
28 NUMBER OF VISITS TO THE PHILIPPINES ☑ 1 ☐ 2 ☐ 3 or more
29 TRAVELING ON PACKAGE TOUR? 1 ☐ YES 2 ☑ NO
32 SIGNATURE OF PASSENGER: Hong
19 AIRPORT OF ORIGIN: INCHEON
18 FLIGHT NO.: KE 621

FOR PHILIPPINE OVERSEAS CONTRACT WORKERS / BALIKBAYAN USE ONLY
OCW I.D. NO.
DATE OF LAST DEPARTURE (MM / DD / YY)
REASONS FOR RETURNING TO RP: 1 ☐ CONTRACT TERMINATED 2 ☐ VACATION / ON LEAVE 3 ☐ HEALTH 4 ☐ OTHERS (SPECIFY)

WARNING: DEATH TO DRUG TRAFFICKERS UNDER PHILIPPINE LAW (RA 7659)

태국 입국 신고서

ตม.6 บัตรขาเข้า
TM.6 ARRIVAL CARD
Thai Immigration Bureau

โปรดเขียนตัวบรรจง และทำเครื่องหมาย ☒
PLEASE WRITE CLEARLY IN BLOCK LETTERS AND MARK ☒

1 ชื่อสกุล Family Name: HONG
18 เที่ยวบินหรือพาหนะอื่น Flight or Other Vehicle No.: KE 651
2 ชื่อตัวและชื่อรอง First Name and Middle Name: GIL DONG
3 สัญชาติ Nationality: KOREA
7 ☑ ชาย Male ☐ หญิง Female
12 เลขที่หนังสือเดินทาง Passport No.: JR123456
4 วัน-เดือน-ปีเกิด Date of Birth: 01 01 1960 (dd mm yyyy)
16 ตรวจลงตราเลขที่ Visa No.:
26 ที่อยู่ในประเทศไทย Address in Thailand: ABC HOTEL 48 ORINTAL AVE. BANGKOK
สำหรับเจ้าหน้าที่/For official use
BF 30269
32 ลายมือชื่อ Signature: Hong
เฉพาะชาวต่างชาติกรุณากรอกข้อมูลบนบัตรทั้ง 2 ด้าน
For non-Thai resident, Please complete on both sides of this card

러시아 입국 신고서

МИГРАЦИОННАЯ КАРТА

Серия 05 05 № 025014

1 Фамилия: HONG

2 Имя: GIL DONG

Отчество

4 Дата рождения: День 01 Месяц 01 Год 1960 — 7 Пол: Муж / Жен

12 Документ, удостоверяющий личность: JR123456 — 3 Гражданство: KOREA

22 Цель визита (нужное подчеркнуть): Служебный визит, Туризм, Коммерческий визит, Учёба, Работа, Частный визит, Транзит

30 Сведения о приглашающей стороне (наименование физического или юридического лица, адрес): TRAVEL AGENCY, PUSHKIN STREET 10/2

16 Идентификационный номер визы: JR123456

31 Номер приглашения на въезд: IH123456

Срок пребывания: 25 с: 01.12.2005 до: 05.12.2005 — 32 Подпись: Hong

Служебные отметки

Въезд в Российскую Федерацию	Выезд из Российской Федерации

Регистрация и изменение срока временного пребывания в Российской Федерации

미국입국카드(arrival card (US))

U.S. Department of Justice
Immigration and Naturalization Service — OMB 1115-0077

Admission Number — 미국방문을 환영합니다.

591015031 12

I-94 본 서식 작성 요령

미국시민권자, 영주권 소유 외국인, 이민비자 소지자, 캐나다 시민권자를 제외한 모든 방문객은 이 양식을 기입해 주십시오.
타자 또는 정자로 읽기좋게 전부 대문자로 쓰십시오. 영어를 사용 하십시오. 이 양식의 뒷면은 쓰지 마십시오.
이 양식은 이부로 나누어져 있습니다. 도착기록(항목 1부터 13까지)과 출발기록(항목 14부터 17까지)양쪽을 전부 기입해 주십시오.
이 항목을 다 기입하신후 이 양식을 미국 이민국 검사관에게 제출 하십시오.
항목-7 육로로 미국에 입항하면, LAND라고 이 공란에 기입하십시오. 선박편으로 미국에 입항할 때는 SEA라고 이 공란에 기입하십시오.
Form I-94 (05-09-90)N

Admission Number — 영문 대문자로 기재하십시오 (WRITE IN ENGLISH ONLY)

591015031 12

Immigration and Naturalization Service
I-94
Arrival Record (도착기록)

1. 성(姓): HONG	
2. 이름: GIL DONG	3. 생일(일/월/년): 01 01 60
4. 국적: KOREA	5. 성별(남, 여)
6. 여권번호: JR123456	7. 항공사 및 항공편명: KE017
8. 현재 주재국: KOREA	9. 탑승한 장소(도시명): SEOUL
10. 비자를 발행한 장소(도시명): SEOUL	11. 발행날자(일/월/년): 01 01 05
12. 미국에 체류기간 중 주소(번지·거리): 1813 WILSHIRE BOULEVARD	
13. 시 및 주: LOS ANGELES, CA90057	

Departure Number

591015031 12

Immigration and Naturalization Service
I-94
Departure Record (출발기록)

14. 성(姓): HONG	
15. 이름: GIL DONG	16. 생일(일/월/년): 01 01 60
17. 국적: KOREA	

뒷쪽을 보시오. KOREAN — KOREAN AIR — STAPLE HERE

한국세관신고서카드(customs declaration card (Korea)

CUSTOMS DECLARATION

KOREA CUSTOMS SERVICE

All arriving travelers (including crew members) must complete and sign this Customs Declaration form and hand it to a Customs officer. You may be questioned and inspected to verify the information you have provided. Family members traveling together may complete one 「Customs Declaration」

Name (Last) (First) (Middle)				Birth Date (day / mo. / yr.)
Passport No.	Nationality	Occupation	☐ Male ☐ Female	Family Members
Address while in Korea			Phone ( )	
Entry Date (day/mo./yr.)	Airline / Flight No. or Vessel Name KE	Purpose of Visit ☐ Tour ☐ Business ☐ Others		Length of Stay days

◇ **Travelers with goods to declare** If you have any of the following articles, check the appropriate box, provide further information on reverse side, and hand this Declaration to a Customs officer at the 「Goods to Declare」 channel.

☞ If you make a voluntary declaration of dutiable items, your customs clearance will be prompt, and inspection will generally not be required. Residents need not pay immediately: post-clearance duty payment will allow you to pay within 15 days of receiving the Duty Payment Notice.

☐ 1. Goods purchased or acquired outside Korea (including goods received free of charge), or goods purchased in duty free stores in Korea and brought back into Korea. Exclude personal effects which have been used or worn prior to the time of arrival and are generally recognized as travel articles.

☐ 2. Any gemstone, pearl, tortoiseshell, coral, amber, ivory, or their products exceeding US$600 in value among item 1 goods. (Any of these which are US$600 or less in value should be categorized as item 1)

☐ 3. More than 1 bottle (not over 1 liter) of alcoholic beverages: more than 200 cigarettes (50 cigars, or 250 grams of tobacco) ; or more than 2 ounces of perfume among item 1 goods. (If you are under 20 years of age, you must declare all alcoholic beverages and tobacco products.)

☐ 4. Commercial goods for sale

☐ 5. Weapons (including mock and ornamental weapons), such as firearms and knives or any explosive or poisonous substances

☐ 6. Narcotics, psychotropic substances, or their products

☐ 7. Articles harmful to the national constitution, public security or morals (e.g., books, publications, photographs, video tapes, films, LD, CD, CD-ROM, etc.)

☐ 8. Altered, forged or counterfeited currency or banknotes

☐ 9. Animals: agricultural, forestry, livestock or marine products: or CITES-protected animals, plants, or their products

☐ 10. Foreign currency or other monetary instruments exceeding US$10,000 or Korean currency exceeding ₩8,000,000 (including personal checks, travelers checks, etc.)

＊ Items 5-10 can be cleared after declation has been made, or if prior permission has been obtained from the appropriate ministry.

◇ **Visitor's (non-resident's) goods which will be taken out of Korea upon departure**

Declare the total quantity and amount on reverse side for duty exemption

＊ Goods which will be/have been contributed to/from governments or international organizations are duty free. You do not need to declare these goods

◇ **Travelers with item 1 goods totalling US$400 or less and no other items to declare**

Check the box below and hand this Declaration to a Customs officer at the 「Nothing to Declare」 channel. You do not need to complete the reverse side.

☞ Making false declarations or failing to declare item 1 goods exceeding US$400 in value or prohibited or restricted goods may result in civil penalties and/or criminal prosecution under the Customs Law, Foreign Exchange Management Law, Firearms & Chemicals Enforcement Law, Narcotics & Psychotropic Substance Control Law, etc.

☐ Item 1 goods totalling US$400 or less and no other items to declare

Traveler's Signature :

473-06821인
96. 9. 5 승인

More Announcements [5]

1. Routine Announcements

BOARDING & BAGGAGE SECURING

Ladies and gentlemen,
this is Asiana Airlines / flight _______ bound for ___________.
Please check your flight number.

The use of electronic devices /[6] such as mobile phones is not allowed / at any time during the flight.
Please turn off your mobile phone / and other electronic devices.
Also, please keep all carry-on baggage / in the overhead bins / or under the seat in front of you. Thank you

WELCOME

Good morning (or afternoon/evening), / ladies and gentlemen.
Captain ______ and the entire crew / would like to welcome you aboard / Asiana Airline flight ________ / bound for _________.

Our flight time will be _____ hour(s) ____ minutes / following take-off. Please make sure / your seat belt is securely fastened.
And please return your seat back and tray table / to their upright position.
The use of electronic devices / including a mobile phone is not

5) 이동희. Alan Parsons, Airline Practical English (서울:새로미, 2006), pp.158-188
6) /는 방송시 끊어서 읽을 곳을 표시합니다.

allowed / during take–off and landing.

Smoking in the cabin and lavatories / is prohibited at all times / during the flight.
We're pleased / to have you on board today / and we'll do our very best / to serve you. Thank you.

TAKE-OFF

Ladies and gentlemen, / we'll be taking off shortly.
Please make sure / your seat belt is securely fastened.
Thank you.

SAFETY DEMONSTRATION

Ladies and gentlemen, / please review the safety instruction card / in your seat pocket.
Thank you.

SEAT BELT SIGN-OFF

Ladies and gentlemen, / although the seat belt sign has been turned off, / in case of sudden turbulence, / please keep your seat belt fastened / at all times during the flight.

> We recommend that you keep your seat belt fastened during the flight.

We'd like to remind you / that smoking is prohibited in the cabin / and lavatories.
Your cooperation is much appreciated. Thank you.

DUTY-FREE SALES

Ladies and gentlemen, / in a few minutes, we'll begin our of sales of duty free items.
If you'd like to purchase any items,

○ ORDER BASIS

Please fill out the order form / in your seat pocket and give it to your flight attendant.

○ CART BASIS

Please let us know / as the duty–free sales cart passes by your seat.
We accept US dollars, ____ , and _______.

The duty–free allowances for (Country name) are / _____liter(s) of liquor, (Cartons / packs) of cigarettes for (visitors / residents) and __ ounces of perfume.

For your convenience, / we have a pre–order form which will allow you to order items / and pick them up on your return flight.

For further information, please contact your flight attendants. Thank you.

SHORT SUBJECT & MOVIE SHOWING

○ SHORT SUBJECT

Ladies and gentlemen, /
we'll be showing you broadcasts of / KBS news and CNN news / from Nov 4.

In a few minutes, / we will be showing you a short video program, / "______" followed by "______"

Please turn to channel 1 for English / or 2 for Korean.
Thank you.

○ MOVIE SHOWING

Ladies and gentlemen, /
in a few minutes, / we'll be showing you (a/two) movie(s).

in a few minutes, / we'll be showing you our (first) movie titled / with______. The second movie is _____ with _____.

Snacks and refreshments are available at all times.

We hope you enjoy the movie(s). Thank you.

DOCUMENTATION

Ladies and gentlemen, / upon entering Korea, / please have your passport / and other entry documents ready.

All nationalities are required to fill out the Arrival card.

Passengers who have baggage / arriving on another aircraft or by ship / must fill out two customs forms.

2. Irregular Announcements

DELAYED DEPARTURE (1)

Ladies and gentlemen, / we'll be (or we're) delayed /

1. due to air traffic.
2. due to aircraft servicing.
3. due to dense fog (or heavy rain / heavy snow / strong wind etc.) at _____ International Airport.
4. due to snow removal on the runway.

1. We'll be departing in about _____hour(s) and _____ minutes.
2. We'll depart as soon as possible.

We appreciate your understanding and patience. Thank you.

DELAYED DEPARTURE (2)

Ladies and gentlemen, / we're now waiting for /

1. our turn to take off.
2. the completion / of check–in procedures by passengers.
3. the completion / of baggage (or cargo) loading.
4. the departure (or take–off) clearance.
5. passenger / from a connecting flight.

SAFETY DEMONSTRATION

◯ Video Showing

Ladies and gentlemen, / we'd like to familiarize you / with the safety features of this aircraft.
Please take a moment / to view the following video program.
Thank you.

RETURN FROM A TAXIWAY

Ladies and gentlemen, we must return to the terminal area /

1. due to maintenance / of the aircraft.
2. due to the orders / from the control tower.
3. due to a sick passenger.
4. ....

We appreciate your understanding and patience. Thank you.

DELAYED DEPARTURE DUE TO THE WEATHER CONDITION

1.

Ladies and gentlemen, /
the take–off (landing) conditions at ____ International Airport / are unsatisfactory due to dense fog (or heavy rain / heavy snow / strong wind / dust storms etc.), / our departure will be delayed.
Further information will be provided to you shortly. Thank you.

2.

Ladies and gentlemen, / the weather conditions at ______ International Airport / have not improved yet.

1. We expect to depart in about ____hour(s) and _____ minutes.
2. A decision will be made / following the ____o'clock weather check.

Thank you for your understanding and patience.

3.

Ladies and gentlemen, /
the weather conditions at ______ International Airport / have improved.
We expect to depart in about _____hour(s) and _____ minutes.
Thank you.

FLIGHT CANCELLATION / DELAYED OPERATION

Ladies and gentlemen, /
we regret to announce / that this flight has been cancelled (delayed) /

1. due to the bad weather conditions / at ______ International Airport.
2. due to runway closure / at _____ International Airport.
3. due to maintenance / of the aircraft.

All passengers are kindly requested to exit / and follow the guidance of our ground staff (or a flight attendant).
Please take all of your belongings with you / when you deplane.

Your cooperation is much appreciated. Thank you.

TURBULENCE

1.
Ladies and gentlemen, /

1. we're expecting some turbulence.
2. we're experiencing some turbulence.

Please fasten your seat belt / and keep it fastened / until the captain turns off the seat belt sign.
Also, passengers traveling with children, / please make sure / your seat belts are securely fastened. Thank you.

2.

As we're experiencing turbulence, / the beverage (or meal) service will not be available.

We'll be continuing our meal (or beverage) service / as soon as the turbulence subsides.

Thank you.

DIVERSION DURING THE FLIGHT

Ladies and gentlemen, /

the weather conditions at ____ International Airport /

have made it impossible for us to land.

1. We're now heading for ____ International Airport / and will arrive in ____ hour(s) and _____ minutes.
2. We're now returning to ____ International Airport / and will arrive in ____ hour(s) and _____ minutes.

We'll do our best / to get you to your destination / as soon as possible. Thank you.

EMERGENCY (1)

Ladies and gentlemen, /
one of our passengers needs urgent medical attention.

1. We'll have to make an unscheduled landing / at ____ International Airport.
2. We'll have to return to ____ International Airport.

Further information will be provided / as it becomes available.
We appreciate your understanding. Thank you.

EMERGENCY (2)

May I have your attention, please? We have a sick passenger.
If there's a doctor / or anyone with medical training on board, /
please contact a flight attendant immediately. Thank you.

AFTER DIVERSION (1)

Ladies and gentlemen, /
the captain has been informed / that the conditions at ____ International Airport / have improved.

We've altered our course / and we're now en-route to ____ International Airport, / our original destination.

We expect to arrive in ____ hour(s) and ____ minutes. Thank you.

AFTER DIVERSION (2)

Ladies and gentlemen, /
we've landed at _____ International Airport /

1. due to the bad weather conditions / at ____ International Airport.
2. due to a sick passenger.
3. due to runway closure / at ____ International Airport.
4. due to maintenance / of the aircraft.

All passengers are kindly requested to remain on board.
Your cooperation is much appreciated. Thank you.

AFTER DIVERSION (3)

Thank you for waiting, / ladies and gentlemen.

1. The weather at _____ International Airport / has improved / and we have received permission ____ / to continue our flight as scheduled.
2. Maintenance has been completed.
3. The passenger has been transported / to a nearby medical facility.
4. The runway at ____ International Airport / has been opened.

We're ready to continue our flight / bound for _____.

Our flight time will be ____ hour(s) and _____ minutes / following take-off.

Please make sure / your seat belt is securely fastened.

Please return your seat back and tray table / to their upright position.

The use of electronic devices / including mobile phones is not allowed / during take-off and landing.

Smoking in the cabin and lavatories / is prohibited at all times / during the flight.

If there's anything / we can do for you, / please let us know.

Thank you.

CIRCLING

Ladies and gentlemen, /

we're now circling _____ International Airport / as we wait for the landing clearance.

The captain has informed us / that landing conditions at ____ International Airport / are unsatisfactory /

1. due to dense fog.
2. due to heavy traffic.
3. due to an aircraft accident.
4. due to runway closure.

Further information will be provided / as it becomes available.

We appreciate your understanding and patience. Thank you.

PAGING

May I have your attention, please?
Would Mr. (or Mrs./Miss) ______, / Mr. (or Mrs. /Miss) ______, please contact our flight attendant (our ground staff) / when you deplane.
Thank you.